THE AGNOSTIC SPIRIT AS A COMMON MOTIF
IN LIBERAL THEOLOGY AND
LIBERAL SCEPTICISM

Editorial Inquiries:

Mellen Research University Press
534 Pacific Avenue
San Francisco, California 94133

Order Fulfillment:

The Edwin Mellen Press
Box 450
Lewiston, New York 14092

THE AGNOSTIC SPIRIT AS A COMMON MOTIF IN LIBERAL THEOLOGY AND LIBERAL SCEPTICISM

James Woelfel

MELLEN RESEARCH UNIVERSITY PRESS
San Francisco

BL
2747.2
. W64
1990

Library of Congress Cataloging in-Publication Data

This book has been registered with the Library of Congress.

ISBN 0-7734-9921-0

Copyright © 1990 James Woelfel

Printed in the United States of America

For Sarah

. . .Personal attachment is a very happy foundation for
friendship. . . .Friendship is a serious affection; the most sublime of
all affections, because it is founded on principle, and cemented by
time.

Mary Wollstonecraft,
A Vindication of the Rights of Woman

Contents

Preface

The essays in this volume have as their common theme the richly dialectical and intimate connections, at the levels of both thought and sensibility, between undogmatic skeptics and liberal Christians of the past hundred years. I discuss their shared sense of metaphysical ignorance and uncertainty in terms of what I call the "agnostic spirit," an attitude of mind having its roots in the philosophical revolutions of Hume and Kant, the progress and influence of the natural sciences, and the development of modern critical historiography and the social sciences. I consider this attitude perhaps the single most important motif in the critical religious thought and the criticism of religion in our time. In my own recent research I have been devoting special attention to the remarkable dialogue between liberalizing Christian thinkers and writers and sympathetic skeptics in Victorian Britain, in the context of which Thomas Henry Huxley coined the term "agnostic" in 1869.

A central theme of my research in the philosophy of religion and in historical and constructive theology since the beginning of my career has been the exploration of the relationships between modern religious belief and unbelief from the standpoint of one who has occupied the "borderlands" between them. Three of my previous books--*Borderland Christianity*, *Albert Camus on the Sacred and the Secular*, and *Augustinian Humanism*--and a number of my articles examine various aspects of the issues generated. The essays included here, almost all of them written during the past five years, represent the most recent directions my thought has been taking, and I have found in the "agnostic spirit" that characterizes both liberal Christianity and open-minded skepticism a unifying interpretative perspective.

A special focus of several of the essays included here is the role of socio-cultural and personal factors in the wide variety of choices people make about both belief and unbelief, and their specific implications for the dialogue between liberal religion and religious skepticism. My observations show the influence of William James and a generally pragmatist approach in acknowledging that a variety of foundationally different perspectives on life can and in fact often do function in human lives to yield similarly humane values, and that contextual and dispositional elements play an important role at the levels of both foundations and fruits. My emphasis on the difficulty--indeed, the impossibility--of definitively adjudicating among the truth-claims of a variety of reasoned forms of religion and skepticism does not, however, reflect an espousal of the currently fashionable epistemological, axiological, and cultural relativisms. While I indicate that the affirmation of universal truths and values must be profoundly shaped and chastened by the relativizing insights of influential twentieth-century schools of thought, I do not mean to imply that I accept their conclusions. The problem is that I have yet to find a self-consistent relativism. The coherence of the various relativisms is belied by the very attempt to formulate them as presumably universal theories, by internal contradictions, and by the inability of the persons holding them to carry them out consistently in concrete judgments about the world and human action. The impossibility of resolving differences among a number of reasoned interpretations of reality arises instead simply from inherent limitations of human knowledge. That is why an agnostic frame of mind is appropriate to issues of religion. Within this framework, however, it is both theoretically illuminating and of practical benefit to explore, as James did, the intellectual, moral, aesthetic, and religious values that are often the common fruit of differing "ultimate concerns."

While I broadly characterize in Chapter Four what I mean by "liberal faith" in the book's subtitle, perhaps I should say a word about "liberal doubt" here. I refer to forms of doubt or skepticism that are open to, sympathetic with, and not infrequently even nostalgic about, at least some forms of Christianity or certain Christian claims. I would contrast liberal doubt with intellectually dogmatic and/or religiously indifferent forms of atheism and agnosticism. It is precisely this liberal doubt that has been so closely involved with the deeply agnostic tendencies that have characterized critical forms of Christianity in the past hundred years.

I want to emphasize that this collection of essays reflects a commonality-in-diversity. They were written at different times, with varying purposes, and for a range of readers or auditors. In each essay (except for Chapter One, the "programmatic" essay) I examine a specific issue and approach things from a somewhat different angle. The careful reader will undoubtedly find both linguistic and substantive inconsistencies among the essays along the way. At the same time, I trust that the careful reader will also discern the repeated themes, methods, references, and conclusions that I believe give this volume its unity and coherence as a multi-faceted exploration of the "agnostic spirit" in modern thought on religion.

Four of the essays are revised versions of articles that have appeared previously. "Humane Vision: Theological Norm and Dialogical Platform" appeared in *Encounter* 49:4, Autumn 1988, 321-335; and "The Personal Dimension in Theological Inquiry" in *Encounter* 42:3, Summer 1981, 225-233. "The Future of American Religious Thought: A Critical Perspective" was published in *Ultimate Reality and Meaning: Interdisciplinary Studies in the Philosophy of Understanding* 8:4, December 1985, 288-298. "Indwelling and Exile: Two Types of Religious and Secular World-Orientation" first appeared in the *American Journal of Theology and Philosophy* 8:3, September 1987, 93-108. I acknowledge with thanks their editors' permission to reprint them in revised form.

I want also to express my appreciation to audiences who heard the original versions of four of the essays and especially to those who asked hard questions and made useful criticisms. I presented "The Agnostic Motif in Modern Thought and Sensibility" to the participants in the St. Mary's College Summer School of Theology at the University of St. Andrews in July of 1989. "American Feminist Theology and the American Pragmatist Tradition" and "Victorian Agnosticism and Liberal Theology" were originally papers presented at the 1988 and 1989 national meetings of the American Academy of Religion. My colleagues in Philosophy heard a very preliminary draft of "Humane Vision" at a monthly departmental colloquium in 1987.

Work on some of the essays was supported by grants from the General Research Fund of the University of Kansas in 1986 and 1988. A sabbatical leave from the university in the spring semester of 1990 enabled me to bring this book to completion and prepare it for publication. I am grateful to the faculty research and sabbatical leave committees for their confidence in my proposals. I also acknowledge with appreciation financial assistance in connection with publication from the university's Scholarly Publication Revolving Fund. To Pam Lerow and her staff at the College Word Processing Center I am indebted for their patience and high-quality efforts in producing the camera-ready copy. I want in addition to thank my good friend Karen Humburg for her careful and professional proofreading of several chapters.

The essays included here come out of a period of my life that has been immeasurably enriched by my partnership with Sarah Chappell Trulove. Our marriage has been the true friendship Mary Wollstonecraft praised as the enduring virtue of marriage. It has also been a stimulating intellectual companionship of joint research and editing ventures and of growth and new directions for each of us. To her this book is dedicated with love, respect, and appreciation.

Lawrence, Kansas
July, 1990

Chapter 1

The Agnostic Motif in Modern Thought and Sensibility

An increasingly important motif in the past hundred years of critical thought on religion in the West, among believers and skeptics alike, has been the widespread acknowledgment of significant limitations on human knowledge. Confident atheisms on the one hand, and the theological assurances of previous centuries on the other, have been out of favor for some time. They have been replaced among both critics of Christianity and Christian writers by a sense of metaphysical uncertainty and ignorance that expresses itself both in their intellectual assumptions and methods and in a range of sensibilities. This agnostic spirit is rooted in the epistemological critiques of Hume and Kant and has articulated itself in a variety of forms in philosophy, theology, and literature.

I believe that the agnostic frame of mind is perhaps more than any other single feature definitive of what we have come to think of as "modernity" in religious thought and critical thought on religion. It has manifested itself, among many reflective humanists and theists, in a remarkable blurring of the boundaries between belief and unbelief and a common recognition that any sort of definitive answers to "ultimate questions" eludes our grasp. What we often find, in examining the literature, is an intellectual dialogue that includes on the one hand Christian thinkers whose assumptions and uncertainties are scarcely distinguishable from those of sympathetic skeptics, and on the other hand skeptics who write sensitively and appreciatively of the affirmations of faith.

I want to begin with the origins and definition of the term "agnostic." Then I will offer a general characterization of post-Kantian philosophical and religious thought to call attention to how widely prevalent what we might call the "uncertainty principle"--to use the name of a physical theory as a general metaphor--has become. In that connection I also want to indicate how the agnostic spirit manifests itself in a range of sensibilities. For specific examples of the agnostic motif among both Christian thinkers and their skeptical critics, I will go on to focus on a few British and North American philosophers of religion of recent decades. I will conclude with some reflections on Christian theology. In taking on so general a survey I will be painting with a wide brush. I hope the reader will indulge me in my sweeping generalizations, and bear in mind that I too recognize that in a more detailed study all sorts of distinctions and qualifications would have to be made.

The eminent Victorian biologist and man of letters Thomas Henry Huxley coined the term "agnostic" in 1869 to describe his own views on a number of metaphysical and theological questions. Huxley offered an explicit definition of agnosticism in his essay "Agnosticism and Christianity." He characterized agnosticism, not as a specific viewpoint or set of ideas, but as a general attitude of mind that could manifest itself in a rich variety of ways. Agnosticism, he said, was simply adherence to the principle that we should reserve judgment or be skeptical about confident assertions of a number of theological (and also metaphysical) claims, on the grounds that the evidence available to us is simply insufficient to provide a basis for reasonable belief.

What, then, is the spirit, mentality, frame of mind, or attitude which since Huxley we have come to call "agnostic," and which I am contending is characteristic of much of the critical humanism and the critical theism of the past hundred years? As we have seen, Huxley put an "alpha privative" in front of the word "gnostic" to indicate that the agnostic is one who professes not to have knowledge sufficient to decide about a range of theological and metaphysical affirmations and alternatives. According to his contemporary R. H. Hutton, Huxley got the idea from St. Paul's reference to the unknown God (*agnosto theo*) in Acts 17.23. Standard definitions of agnosticism normally link it specifically to an attitude toward the question of the existence of God, and that is certainly the commonest use of the term. Thus we distinguish among theism, as belief in a creator God; atheism, as disbelief in or denial of the existence of God; and agnosticism, as doubt or inability to decide about the existence of God.

But the standard usage and dictionary definitions miss the heart of what Huxley was enunciating and his own recognition of its wide and varied implications. In his 1902 book *Agnosticism* Robert Flint of the University of Edinburgh complained that it was gratuitous of Huxley to invent the word "agnostic" when the word "skeptic" had been around for centuries.[1] But while it is common to use, and I often use, the two terms interchangeably, they seem to me etymologically to point to different aspects of the phenomenon of doubt. "Skeptical" connotes an active calling into question, while the emphasis of "agnostic" is simply a not-knowing, an uncertainty in the face of the evidence available. It is this latter frame of mind that has been widely pervasive in modern thought both secular and religious. Although it has often enough also been accompanied by an active skepticism, it has also frequently been characterized by a sense of wonder and mystery that one does not readily associate with the term "skeptical."

In a manner that I believe is consistent with Huxley's own large-minded and flexible definition of the term he coined, then, I am using the term "agnostic" adjectivally to mean, not a specific position on metaphysical and theological issues, but an attitude of not-knowing, of uncertainty, arising out of a deeply-felt sense of the limitations of human knowledge with regard to the most fundamental human questions. For this reason I try to avoid the term "agnosticism," which as an "-ism" word may too easily suggest a body of belief or world-view, and prefer to speak only of the "agnostic principle" (Huxley's own phrase), or the agnostic attitude, frame of mind, or spirit. However, when I use "agnostic" as a noun I bow to ordinary usage. I mean by it those who, like Huxley, so describe themselves, who stand outside Christianity as critics unable to accept even the liberalized reinterpretations of the gospel that in the twentieth century have exemplified the agnostic spirit within the church. When I occasionally resort to using "agnosticism," I intend it simply as a collective term to designate agnostics and their quite varied views.

---

[1] New York: Charles Scribner's Sons, 4-5.

Before I characterize the agnostic mentality that has characterized much nineteenth- and twentieth-century secular and Christian thought, I want to acknowledge the "agnostic" strain that has been a venerable tradition in Christian theology from its earliest days through the Middle Ages and beyond. I refer to the *via negativa* or apophatic mode of theology of which the literature of mysticism from Pseudo-Dionysius onward is full, but which is also important in the "mainstream" of the theological tradition from Augustine to the present. This reverently agnostic element in Christian thought is rooted, of course, in the apprehension that revelation is precisely the disclosure of the infinite and unfathomable Ground of being which graciously makes itself known to humanity within the limitations of our finite grasp and speech. But for pre-Kantian theology this affirmation of the divine mystery and our unknowing went hand in hand with a considerable degree of assurance about what God has communicated to us, based on the assumption of the trustworthiness of Scripture and Church and often also on an optimism about human reason's purchase on reality. Out of this assurance dogmas could be defined, anathemas pronounced, crusades and inquisitions undertaken, heretics and infidels condemned, the scientific revolution opposed, and religious wars fought between Catholics and Protestants. Would that the agnostic dimension that is at the very heart of the Christian grasp of things had all along played a more central role in Christian thinking and action!

It was with the Enlightenment that the assurances of Christianity, both Protestant and Catholic, began to be seriously challenged. That philosopher who is both an epitome of Enlightenment consciousness and (along with David Hume) a great critic of unexamined Enlightenment assumptions, Immanuel Kant, is the real watershed, with his comprehensive critiques of both theoretical and practical knowledge. To this day the main currents of twentieth-century Protestant thought have remained dominated by two assumptions developed largely from Kant: (1) Theoretical knowledge is restricted to the phenomenal world of nature, thereby making impossible the "natural" or metaphysical theology that had been so important a part of the Christian intellectual tradition. (2) The assertions of religion, like those of morality, belong to the practical sphere of life (broadly conceived), and are specifically grounded in the language of self-awareness, personal agency, and human relations.

Kant's "Copernican Revolution" in epistemology and metaphysics was followed by the romantic movement, elements of which emphasized the role of intuition and feeling in human life and criticized the Enlightenment's excessive confidence in reason. Schleiermacher, the father of modern liberal theology, belongs to romanticism as surely as do Wordsworth and Emerson. Historical-critical study of the biblical literature, which emerged to prominence by the middle of the nineteenth century, was of course absolutely crucial in shaping subsequent theological developments by undercutting traditional claims of divinely-assured trustworthiness regarding the biblical texts. Advances in the natural sciences, above all evolutionary theory, were likewise centrally important in producing the chastened theological mentality of the past hundred years. The rise of social-scientific study of religion in the work of investigators such as Auguste Comte, Emile Durkheim, and Sir James Frazer, together with the growing knowledge of other religions and the availability of their sacred texts, all had the effect of relativizing the absolute claims of Christianity. Historical studies generally gave impetus to a historical relativism that challenged theologians and positively shaped the work of such influential religious thinkers as Ernst Troeltsch.

The impact of these familiar intellectual developments cannot be overestimated in any attempt to understand the sea-change that has taken place in religious reflection in the last hundred years. It was precisely these challenges that persuaded some eminent Victorian thinkers and writers to break away--often with great anguish--from the Christianity in which they had been raised. The stories of noted Victorian agnostics such as Huxley, Arthur Hugh Clough, George Eliot, Leslie Stephen, Harriet Martineau, and Henry Sidgwick, display the full pathos of the changes that were taking place.

Theologians responded both positively and negatively to the unprecedented challenges. Some took the view that believers were confronted with an absolute either/or: they must choose between the old faith and the new knowledge. This was the beginning of fundamentalism. Those theologians who believed it essential for Christianity to embrace, and revise itself in the light of, the new knowledge, did so with greater or lesser enthusiasm, ranging in their accommodation from liberal to conservative. But most who responded positively shared a new humility and caution, a sitting lightly to some previous certainties, an agnostic spirit in the face of the scientific, socio-cultural, and historical evidence and the philosophical critiques of metaphysical knowledge-claims.

Late-nineteenth- and twentieth-century developments in Christian thought have gone hand in hand with and been substantially influenced by post-Kantian trends in philosophy, and I do not believe we can fully grasp the character and problems of the former without understanding something of the latter. It is not much of an exaggeration to say that most of the leading philosophical movements of the late nineteenth and the twentieth centuries have, in a rich variety of ways, continued and elaborated the epistemologically and metaphysically agnostic legacies of Hume and Kant. The Neo-Kantian tradition produced Hans Vaihinger's philosophy of "as if," in which religious and metaphysical ideas were understood as useful fictions. Hume's influence has been considerable in nineteenth- and twentieth-century British philosophy, from the expansive empiricism of John Stuart Mill to the narrow phenomenalism of the logical positivists.

Three of the leading philosophical movements of the twentieth century have been pragmatism, existentialism, and analytic philosophy. Broadly speaking, both the existentialists and the pragmatists were not only anti-rationalists but also anti-foundationalists. In different ways they suggested that there are no universal rational foundations upon which to ground human knowledge. All our beliefs and values are human constructions reflecting human interests and desires, relative to our life-situation or social and cultural "communities of discourse," and validated by their instrumental value in helping us make sense of or give meaning to our world. Within the British analytic tradition the Wittgenstein of the *Philosophical Investigations* came to a similar view, analyzing the various spheres of life and knowledge as different "language games" expressive of different human practices or "forms of life," each with its own internal coherence and its own rules for determining the meaningful, the true and the false. Recent developments in philosophy, such as deconstruction and the "neo-pragmatism" of Richard Rorty, have elaborated further variations on this dominant anti-foundationalist and relativist theme.

These varied epistemological perspectives provide impressive common testimony to the agnostic motif in modern thought. In varied ways they all affirm that human knowledge is not only limited but context-dependent, and that apodictic certainty about anything is an unattainable ideal. Indeed, these twentieth-century philosophical movements can be seen as having taken Humean and Kantian skepticism well beyond Hume and Kant. Significantly, many Protestant theologians of the twentieth century have either allied themselves with or been influenced by one or another of these philosophical movements.

The agnostic spirit has manifested itself not only in these chastened epistemological forms but also in a wide range of sensibilities. In his essays of the 1880s and 1890s, notably "The Will to Believe," William James characterized the agnostic critics of Christianity in his day--people like Huxley and the mathematician W. K. Clifford--as strident exponents of a narrow scientism and materialism. James's monochromatic portrait ignored the range of both ideas and sensibilities among the Victorian agnostics.[2] The fact is that the agnostic frame of mind, even and especially among religious skeptics, has incarnated itself in a variety of basic moods regarding the world and one's place in it. Thus we have, for example, the brisk confidence of George Jacob Holyoake, an indefatigable leader of nineteenth-century British free thought: "The principles of Secularism assert principles to be acted upon. They are affirmative, not negative. . . .Theism and Atheism are. . .avoided as bases of Secular belief. Secularism confines itself to propositions of immediate proof."[3] In sharp contrast is the religiously nostalgic humanism that runs throughout George Eliot's fiction, which for me appears with particular clarity and poignancy in her early story *Janet's Repentance*.[4] As she later wrote, "I have too profound a conviction of the efficacy that lies in all sincere faith, and the spiritual blight that comes with no faith, to have any negative propagandism in me. In fact, I have very little sympathy with Freethinkers as a class, and have lost all interest in mere antagonism to religious doctrines."[5]

In the twentieth century the Spanish-American philosopher George Santayana combined a wide-ranging skepticism with a profound appreciation of the

---

[2]See James Woelfel, "William James on Victorian Agnosticism: A Strange Blindness," in Creighton Peden and Larry Axel, eds., *God, Values, and Empiricism* (Macon, GA: Mercer University Press, 1989), 239-248.

[3]*The Reasoner*, 30:1, January 1871, 1.

[4]In *Scenes of Clerical Life* (New York: Oxford University Press, 1988), 169-301.

[5]Quoted by F. Sydney Morris in *The Agnostic: A Journal of Liberal Thought*, May 1885, 214.

value of religion, as in his book *Reason in Religion*.6 His Olympian serenity contrasts sharply with Albert Camus's passionate existentialist engagement with Christianity as he sought to remain faithful to the earth and humanity in the face of what he called the "enigma" of existence. In Camus's novel *The Plague*, Dr. Bernard Rieux refuses to regard his own unbelief as unusual or heroic. Responding to Tarrou's question whether he believes in God, Rieux replies, "No-- but what does that really mean? I'm fumbling in the dark, struggling to make something out. But I've long ceased finding that original."7 And like many of the great Victorian doubters, the twentieth-century British poet Stevie Smith sensitively expressed the conflict in herself as one who had grown up in the church but could not accept its certainties: "My thoughts about Christianity are much confused by my feelings. My feelings fly up, my thoughts draw them down again, crying: Fairy stories. But how can one's heart *not* go out to the idea that a God of absolute love is in charge of the universe, and that in the end, All will be well?"8 Just as the agnostic spirit is no one set of ideas, neither does it express itself in any particular mode of sensibility. It exists in all shades along a spectrum whose end points are a brisk skepticism uninterested in religion at one extreme, and an intensely religious awe and even affirmation at the other.

Now I want briefly to present a few examples out of many I might have chosen to illustrate the agnostic mentality and mood that I am suggesting has been important in the critical theism and the criticism of theism in the twentieth century. I will limit myself to a handful of representatives of British and North American philosophy of religion of the 1950s and 1960s. I do so because I really believe that that was an unusually rich and fruitful period of genuine dialogue on religion between believers and unbelievers in the English-speaking intellectual world. But I could equally well have focussed on the debates of the twenties and thirties between religious liberals and humanists in the U.S. in which figures like John Dewey were

---

6George Santayana, *Works*, vol. IV (New York: Charles Scribner's Sons, 1936).

7Trans. Stuart Gilbert (New York: Alfred A. Knopf, 1948), 116.

8"Some Impediments to Christian Commitment," in *Me Again: Uncollected Writings of Stevie Smith*, ed. by Jack Barbera and William McBrien with a Preface by James MacGibbon (London: Virago Press, 1982), 153.

involved,[9] the controversy aroused in recent years by the radically agnostic reinterpretation of Christianity by Don Cupitt, an Anglican priest and Dean of Emmanuel College of Cambridge University,[10] or other examples.

In his 1958 book *Christianity and Paradox*, Ronald Hepburn described himself as a "sceptic with a naturally religious mind," and spoke of his continuing "personal pilgrimage in search of a satisfactory justification of religious belief."[11] He wrote critically but sympathetically of the main contemporary forms of theological defense, not concluding that God did not exist or that Christianity was not true but rather that the reasons given by sophisticated believers for these affirmations did not hold up to critical scrutiny. In the last chapter of the book Hepburn sought with great earnestness to claim the myths of the Bible and the doctrines of Christianity as humanly insightful parables for the religiously-minded agnostic. He wrote: "If we could show that a great many religious attitudes and experiences can be retained with sincerity, and that religious symbols can continue to have an important part in the life of the sceptic, this would remove the intolerable strain of believing that the ultimate choice is between Christian faith or a life not worth living. . . ."[12]

On the Christian side, Ian Crombie's essay responding to Antony Flew's falsifiability challenge to Christian truth-claims in "Theology and Falsification" remains one of the best of the writings that came out of the renewed philosophy-theology dialogue of the 1950s in Britain. Crombie spoke of the "logical mother" of religious belief, "a response, not precisely logical, and yet in no sense emotional or evaluative, to certain elements in our experience, whose characteristic is that they induce us, not to make straightforward statements about the world, but to strain and distort our media of communication in order to express what we make of them."[13]

---

[9]See, e.g., Henry Nelson Wieman, "John Dewey's Common Faith," *The Christian Century*, Nov. 14, 1934, 1450-1452; and the subsequent debate among Wieman, Dewey, and E. E. Aubrey, "Is John Dewey a Theist?" *The Christian Century*, Dec. 5, 1934, 1550-1553.

[10]See, e.g., his *Taking Leave of God* (London: SCM Press, 1980); *The World to Come* (London: SCM Press, 1982); *Only Human* (London: SCM Press, 1985).

[11](London: Watts, 1958), 1.

[12]P. 191.

[13]"Theology and Falsification," in Antony Flew and Alasdair MacIntyre, eds., *New Essays in Philosophical Theology* (New York: Macmillan, 1955), 115-116.

This "natural theism" provides humans with the subject of their statements about God or the divine. The specific predicates are provided by the "logical father," "the interpretation of certain objects or events as a manifestation of the divine"[14]--in other words, revelation.

Crombie went on to argue that the only language Christianity has to attempt to predicate things of God is the language of "authoritative parable," supremely the biblical stories about Jesus. "What is thus given," he wrote, "is certainly not knowledge of the object to which they apply; it is something much more like a direction. We do not, that is, know to what to refer our parables; we know merely that we are to refer them out of experience, and out of it in which direction. The expression 'God' is to refer to that object, whatever it is, and if there be one, which is such that the knowledge of it would be to us knowledge of the unfamiliar term in the contrast between finite and infinite."[15] Crombie summed up his characterization of the language of Christianity in a striking passage which I think is worth quoting despite its length:

> Much of what I have said agrees very closely with what the atheist says about religious belief, except that I have tried to make it sound better. The atheist alleges that the religious man supposes himself to know what he means by his statements only because, until challenged, he interprets them anthropomorphically; when challenged, however, he retreats rapidly backwards towards complete agnosticism. I agree with this, with two provisos. The first is that the religious man does not suppose himself to know what he means by his statements. . .; he knows what his statements mean within the parable, and believes that they are the right statements to use. (Theology is not a science; it is a sort of art of enlightened ignorance.) The second proviso is that the agnosticism is not complete; for the Christian, under attack, falls back not in any direction, but in one direction; he falls back upon the person of Christ, and the concrete realities of the Christian life.[16]

During the 1950s and 1960s one of the most interesting and "maverick" philosophers in the United States was Walter Kaufmann, for many years a distinguished professor at Princeton. An Austrian whose family fled the Nazis in

---

14P. 116.
15P. 124.
16P. 128.

the late 1930s, he was raised a Lutheran, as a teenager returned to the Jewish heritage of his grandparents, and as an adult was both a vigorously critical and a sympathetic religious skeptic. Achieving eminence as a translator and interpreter of Nietzsche, Kaufmann was a highly original philosopher with a passion for intellectual honesty who was at the same time passionately engaged with the issues of religion. He was a profoundly knowledgeable explorer and critic of Judaism, Christianity, and Buddhism who could write with an insider's sensitivity even as his commitment to honesty kept him an outsider. In his books *Critique of Religion and Philosophy*[17] and *The Faith of a Heretic*,[18] Kaufmann combined devastating exposure of the intellectual and moral foibles of Christian faith, thought, and practice with eloquent appreciation of what he found to be true and noble in the tradition.

Kaufmann liked to quote approvingly this statement of Tolstoy's:

. . ."I divide men. . .into two lots. They are freethinkers, or they are not freethinkers. . . .Freethinkers are those who are willing to use their minds without prejudice and without fearing to understand things that clash with their own customs, privileges, or beliefs. This state of mind is not common, but it is essential for right thinking; where it is absent, discussion is apt to become worse than useless. A man may be a Catholic, a Frenchman, or a capitalist, and yet be a freethinker; but if he put his Catholicism, his patriotism, or his interest, above his reason, and will not give the latter free play where those subjects are touched, he is not a freethinker. His mind is in bondage."[19]

In the context of my general theme, Kaufmann through Tolstoy here articulates an important reason why the agnostic spirit has come to be a defining feature of modern critical thought and sensibility regarding religious belief. Whether we are sympathetic unbelievers like Hepburn and Kaufmann or thoughtful believers like Crombie, the virtues of plain honesty and reason in the face of modern knowledge and--I would add here--of the appalling moral evils and challenges of the twentieth century, have brought us close together in a common sense of our ignorance, our finitude, our vulnerability, and our perpetual penchant for idolatry. Both the

---

[17](Garden City: Doubleday, 1958).
[18](Garden City: Doubleday, 1961).
[19]*Critique of Religion and Philosophy*, 9.

confident theisms and the optimistic humanisms that flourished a hundred years ago
have been shaken to their roots by the ideas and events that have shaped the
twentieth century and who we are.

To my mind perhaps the single most important North American exponent of
this probing agnostic honesty from the Christian side in the 1960s was Michael
Novak, especially in his book *Belief and Unbelief*.[20] Indeed, Novak was one of
the liveliest philosophers of religion in the U.S. during that decade and into the
1970s, exploring issues with philosophical originality, personal integrity, and
literary power in books such as *Belief and Unbelief* and *The Experience of
Nothingness*.[21]

Now the Michael Novak of whom I'm speaking is not to be confused with
the Michael Novak who since 1981 has been a very articulate and aggressive
apologist for political Reaganism and traditionalist Catholicism. Strictly speaking
they are the same person, but any resemblance between the earlier and the later
Novak is purely coincidental!

Novak's unflinching personal candor in *Belief and Unbelief* is reminiscent
of the Anglican theologian and religious Harry Williams, whose writings I also
greatly admire.[22] Raised a Roman Catholic and continuing actively in that
tradition, Novak confessed in his "Foreword" to the book:

> . . .I do not understand God, nor the way in which he
> works. Perhaps there is a heaven, and I will see my brother [a
> priest who was murdered in Pakistan in 1964], together with his
> murderers. That is beyond my ken. I only know that my salvation
> lies in fidelity to conscience, in fidelity to my work, in fidelity to
> those I love, in whatever contribution I can make toward
> diminishing the amount of suffering in this world. I do not think
> about the end; I attend to each task at its appointed time. If,
> occasionally, I raise my heart in prayer, it is to no God I can see, or
> hear, or feel. It is to a God in as cold and obscure a polar night as
> any nonbeliever has known. God is no "extra" in my life. My nose
> is at my tasks. With a naked belief I believe that such fidelity is not
> in vain, not a mere spark of sense in a suffocating universe, but the

---

[20](New York: New American Library, 1965).

[21](New York: Harper & Row, 1970).

[22]See, e.g., "Theology and Self-awareness," in A. R. Vidler, ed., *Soundings:
Essays Concerning Christian Understanding* (Cambridge: At the University Press,
1964), 69-101; *True Christianity* (Springfield, IL: Templegate Publishers, 1975);
and *True Resurrection* (New York: Harper & Row, 1972).

key and important fact within man's range of knowledge. I am
prepared to admit that my belief may be wrong; I set no special store
by it. My obligation is to be faithful to my conscience, and I do not
expect that I would hesitate an instant once it was clear to me that
atheism is a more consistent human policy. A conscience faithful till
death is of more importance than being on a certain side, whether of
belief or unbelief.[23]

An interesting feature of Novak's discussion is that in characterizing the
alternatives of belief and unbelief he simply assumed a narrow definition of
agnosticism and failed to connect its broader implications with his own deeply
agnostic account of both belief and unbelief. But his words elegantly bespeak the
agnostic spirit of which I have been speaking, as in this description: "The believer
who thinks carefully about his belief has placed himself in a darkness as intense as
that of the nonbeliever. His world view and his actions may be different (or they
may not be). But he is no more comforted or consoled than the nonbeliever by the
course of the world or of his life. He does not hold within his fist the mystery of
human life. He is held in darkness by a hidden God."[24]

Novak summed up his study in an "Epilogue" that ended with a lyrical
affirmation of the hidden unity between reflective Christian and humanist:

> . . .The serious nonbeliever and the serious believer. . .share
> a hidden unity of spirit. When both do all they can to be faithful to
> their understanding and to love, and to the immediate task of
> diminishing the amount of suffering in the world, the intention of
> their lives is similar, even though their conceptions of what they are
> doing are different. Such a unity in the intention of two lives seems
> in the end to be more profound than a unity on the conceptual level.

> . . .believer and nonbeliever are both voyagers. In the
> darkness in which the secret courses of human lives lie hidden, men
> are sometimes closer together, sometimes farther apart, than
> appearances indicate. For this reason, many. . .look searchingly
> into the eyes of others, seeking a brother, a sister, who could be
> anywhere. Among us thrives a brotherhood of inquiry and concern,
> even of those who disagree in interpreting the meaning of inquiry--
> the meaning of human spirit--in the darkness in which we live.[25]

23P. 14.
24Pp. 21-22.
25Pp. 164-165.

Unbelievers and believers such as Hepburn, Crombie, Kaufmann, and Novak speak a language and share an attitude that are now commonly understood and accepted, but were in previous centuries exceptional. They are the language and the spirit of religious modernity and--I would add--authenticity that thoughtful Christians and skeptics have both learned to speak and to embody.

In this essay I have tried to define and broadly to explore the development of the agnostic spirit as an important motif in the critical Christian and the skeptical thought of the past hundred years, focusing for illustration on a few out of many thinkers and writers I might have selected. There are many questions to ask and issues requiring more detailed treatment. For example, I myself would want to insist that there is no essential linkage between the agnostic humility on ultimate questions that I believe is demanded by modern knowledge and the extreme epistemological skepticism of some of the chief philosophical fashions of the twentieth century. I can perfectly well be a critical realist, with reasoned confidence that we have sufficient access to objective reality to enable us to test and correct our statements about it, and still recognize that the limitations of our grasp on things prevent us from absolute knowledge of existential matters--above all the ultimate whys and wherefores of our human existence.

In fact, one of my concerns about post-Kantian and especially twentieth-century forms of Protestant theology is the ease and indeed the enthusiasm with which many theologians have wedded themselves--often rather uncritically--to the varieties of epistemological and even moral relativism that have been influential in twentieth-century philosophy. In the face of the challenges of modern knowledge the agnostic temper of Protestant thought has too easily taken refuge in a *fideism* the full implications of which it has usually not been willing to face. Greeting the skepticism of much post-Kantian philosophy with a great sigh of relief, Protestant theologians have too often played the *tu quoque* game to justify Christian faith. I sometimes like to characterize this thoroughgoingly relativistic theological rationale as saying that since there are no good reasons for anything, the fact that there are no good reasons for faith is no criticism and we can happily get on with things. Or, to express it with the judgment pronounced on the caucus race in *Alice in Wonderland*, "All have won, and all shall have prizes." The passion for honesty that is at the very heart of the agnostic frame of mind is not well represented by this sort of easy solution.

Chapter 2

Victorian Agnosticism and Liberal Theology: T. H. Huxley and Matthew Arnold

Two "eminent Victorians," one a skeptic and one a liberal Christian, afford us a kind of paradigm of that "borderland" mentality between critical faith and doubt that has been particularly evident in liberal forms of theology and their sympathetic secular critics. The scientist Thomas Henry Huxley (1820-1895) coined the term "agnostic" in 1869 to describe his own position regarding a number of theological and metaphysical assertions. But not only did he define what would become an important aspect of the thought and sensibility of critical reflection on religion in the twentieth century; he remains one of its most sensitive and open-minded exponents. Huxley actively involved himself in the theological controversies of his day, in which he showed himself to be not only an informed and enlightened critic but also a humane and generous respecter of his opponents. His contemporary and friend, the poet and critic Matthew Arnold (1822-1888), was also a lively participant in theological issues, but as a liberal Anglican who attacked the theologians in an effort to rescue Christianity from obscurantism and irrelevance. In books such as *Literature and Dogma* (1873) Arnold both reflected and anticipated developments in liberal Protestant thought, and in his emphasis on experience, ethics, and humane culture in interpreting the Bible and Christianity he stands at the heart of the liberal tradition.

1. Huxley and the "agnostic principle"

In his essay "Agnosticism" (1889) Huxley recounts why and how he invented the term "agnostic" by telling about his early intellectual development. "When I reached intellectual maturity," he relates,

> and began to ask myself whether I was an atheist, a theist, or a pantheist; a materialist or an idealist; a Christian or a freethinker; I found that the more I learned and reflected, the less ready was the answer; until, at last, I came to the conclusion that I had neither art nor part with any of these denominations, except the last. The one thing in which most of these people were agreed was the one thing in which I differed from them. They were quite sure they had attained a certain "gnosis"--had, more or less successfully, solved the problem of existence; while I was quite sure I had not, and had a pretty strong conviction that the problem was insoluble.[1]

When he later became a member of the celebrated Metaphysical Society, Huxley says, "most of my colleagues were -*ists* of one sort or another. . . .So I took thought and invented what I conceived to be the appropriate title of 'agnostic.' It came into my head as suggestively antithetic to the 'gnostic' of Church history, who professed to know so much about the very things of which I was ignorant. . . ."[2] After Huxley introduced the term to the Metaphysical Society, it caught on quickly--appropriated by many freethinkers as an apt label for their views, and cursed by many theologians and ecclesiastics as atheism or infidelity under another name.

Huxley characterized agnosticism, not as a specific viewpoint or set of ideas, but as a general attitude of mind that could manifest itself in a variety of ways. Agnosticism, he said, is simply adherence to the principle that one should reserve judgment or be skeptical about confident assertions of a number of theological and metaphysical claims, on the grounds that the evidence available to us is insufficient to provide a basis for reasonable belief. As Huxley put it, "it is wrong for a man to say that he is certain of the objective truth of any proposition unless he can produce evidence which logically justifies that certainty."[3] Like most

---

[1]In *Selections from the Essays*, Alburey Castell, ed. (Arlington Heights, IL: AHM Publishing Corporation, 1948), 87

[2]P. 88.

[3]P. 92.

of his Victorian contemporaries who came to call themselves agnostics--but, significantly, also like Arnold, Ritschl, and other liberal theologians--he believed Hume's and Kant's critiques of metaphysics were decisive and held that theoretical reason is limited to the realm of spatio-temporal phenomena. Huxley freely granted that all sorts of beliefs are possible or conceivable as candidates for reality, but he believed that the lack of evidence for them demands in some cases suspension of judgment and in others outright skepticism.

Among the many things I admire about Huxley are the careful, open-minded, and undogmatic way in which he applied what he called the "agnostic principle" to a range of issues, and his willingness to allow others to define the scope and limits of their agnosticism in their own way:

> The extent of the region of the uncertain, the number of the problems the investigation of which ends in a verdict of not proven, will vary according to the knowledge and the intellectual habits of the individual Agnostic. . . .What I am sure about is that there are many topics about which I know nothing; and which, so far as I can see, are out of reach of my faculties. But whether those things are knowable by anyone else is exactly one of those matters which is beyond my knowledge, though I may have a tolerably strong opinion as to the probabilities of the case.[4]

Huxley did not believe that he himself could confidently pronounce on such issues as theism vs. atheism, idealism vs. materialism, and the immortality of the soul, and he seriously doubted that anyone else was in a position to do so. Invoking Bishop Butler's maxim that "probability is the guide of life," Huxley certainly had his opinions on a number of metaphysical and religious questions as to where the preponderance of the evidence pointed. But he always tried carefully to distinguish between doubt and outright denial.

Huxley's appreciation of the spectrum of views on the great issues of philosophy and theology, and his consistent and perceptive application of the agnostic principle to the range of those issues, are amply attested throughout his writings. He really did reject materialism as sharply as he did idealism, and took delight in arguing that strictly speaking Berkeley's epistemology was irrefutable even though unacceptably speculative like its materialist opposite numbers. He was

---

[4]P. 93.

almost contemptuous of Auguste Comte's positivism, which so influenced fellow freethinkers such as George Eliot and Harriet Martineau, saying that Comte combined "scientific incapacity" and "philosophical incompetence."[5] Huxley criticized his friend Herbert Spencer's positing of the "Unknowable," remarking that "If I am to talk about that of which I have no knowledge at all, I prefer the good old word *God*, about which there is no scientific pretence."[6] As for atheism, he remarked that the absurdities of those who think they have demonstrated the existence of God are exceeded only by those who think they have proved that there is no God.[7] He greatly admired and sharply criticized both Descartes the father of rationalism and Hume the ultimate empiricist. In his reflections on science and scientific method, Huxley was refreshingly "modern," with his "Popperian" approach to the nature and progress of science and his critique of the tendency to reify natural laws. In short, Huxley was a highly independent thinker whose "agnostic principle" functioned in both a broadly appreciative and a rigorously critical way.

In allowing that the agnostic frame of mind could express itself across a broad spectrum of opinions and sensibilities, Huxley was willing to recognize it among some of the theologians of his day. He always maintained that the agnostic's quarrel was not with what he called "scientific theology," but with ecclesiasticism, which he called "the championship of a foregone conclusion."[8] While he did not make altogether clear what he meant by "scientific theology," he referred to its practitioners with respect as Christian thinkers who were trying freely and boldly to rethink Christianity in modern and intellectually coherent terms:

> . . .the Agnostic, knowing too well the influence of prejudice and idiosyncrasy, . . .can wish for nothing more urgently than that the scientific theologian should not only be at perfect liberty to thrash out the matter in his own fashion; but that he should, if he can, find flaws in the Agnostic position; and, even if demonstration is not to be had, that he should put, in their full force, the grounds of the conclusions he thinks probable. *The scientific theologian*

---

[5]*The Essence of T. H. Huxley*, selections from his writings edited with several brief introductory essays by Cyril Bibby (New York: St. Martin's Press, 1967), 86.

[6]Quoted by Bibby, p. 66

[7]P. 71.

[8]*Selections from the Essays*, 93-94.

admits the Agnostic principle, however widely his results may differ from those reached by the majority of Agnostics.[9]

Huxley's remarks here remind us that secular agnostics and liberal religious thinkers in Victorian Britain together suffered the hostility of a church establishment and a general populace that were still deeply traditionalist in their religious beliefs and attitudes. Huxley and some of the other Victorian agnostics were sympathetic toward and even supportive of the struggling emergence of liberal theology in Britain in the writings and speeches of thinkers such as Benjamin Jowett, Mark Pattison, and the other contributors to the landmark volume *Essays and Reviews* (1860); Frederick Denison Maurice; F. W. Robertson; Charles Kingsley; and Matthew Arnold. Huxley saw in Christian reinterpreters like these a passion for the honesty he admired as the intellectual virtue *sine qua non*, a conscientious effort to reshape Christian thought and life fully assimilating contemporary challenges such as biblical criticism and Darwinism, and a new humility about the scope of human knowledge whether natural or revealed.

Huxley at one point referred to Henry Mansel of Magdalen College, Oxford, who spent his last years as Dean of St. Paul's Cathedral, as "an eminently agnostic thinker."[10] He had in mind Mansel's controversial 1858 Bampton Lectures, *The Limits of Religious Thought Examined*, in which, building on Sir William Hamilton's philosophy (which had also influenced the young Huxley), Mansel argued that the transcendent is by definition "incognizable and inconceivable" to the human mind. Interestingly, what Huxley failed to see or at least to point out was that the other side of Mansel's metaphysical agnosticism was a theological *fideism* that anticipated what has been a dominant theological response in the twentieth century to the Kantian and post-Kantian critique of reason.

2. Arnold and liberal theology

In the preceding section I have described T. H. Huxley's coining of the term "agnostic," something of the form his own agnostic perspective took, and his sympathy with the efforts of liberal theologians in Victorian Britain. This is the context in which I want to characterize Matthew Arnold's theological views and to

---

[9]P. 94; emphasis added.
[10]P. 86.

compare him with Huxley.

In his definitive recent study *Matthew Arnold and Christianity: His Religious Prose Writings* (to which I am greatly indebted for aspects of my discussion of Arnold), James C. Livingston sees Arnold as an important modern representative of the tradition of Christian humanism.[11] Arnold sought to reconcile and synthesize what he called the Hebraic and the Hellenic elements in Western thought and life--the Christian and classical traditions--as the Renaissance humanists such as Erasmus had sought to do. As an intellectual leader in an age and a country where the forces of modernity were challenging and disrupting traditional verities and values, he sought an integrated vision of science, culture, and Christianity. To those like Huxley whom scientific knowledge had driven outside the church, he argued that what is enduring in Scripture and Christianity is universally verifiable in human experience, and that for most people in a culture moulded by Christianity the secular substitutes being offered them were cold comfort. To theologians and church leaders Arnold proposed an interpretation of the biblical writings and Christian doctrine that reintegrated them into the fullness of modern cultural life. As Livingston writes, "His effort was one of reconstructing a synthesis of the scientific temper with religious and spiritual values in an age of the growing hegemony of science."[12]

Like Huxley, Arnold actively absorbed those intellectual currents that shaped what he called the *Zeitgeist* of the Victorian age and sought creatively to reshape the thinking of the time. He was conversant with German biblical criticism, as for example the work of Strauss and Baur, long before many of his British theological contemporaries, early accepted Darwinian theory, and shared the Neo-Kantian philosophical views that in German liberal Protestantism were replacing the dominance of Hegel. Livingston highlights two aspects of these influences under the headings "evolution and agnosticism":

> The two movements of mind that best characterize English thought in the second half of the nineteenth century are evolution and agnosticism concerning man's knowledge of the ultimate objects of metaphysical and theological belief. Arnold's intellectual development reveals the deep impress of these ideas on his mind and

---

[11](Columbia: University of South Carolina Press, 1986), 187-189.
[12]P. 8.

on his understanding of the directions that any religious reconstruction must take. The two movements are, of course, but the reverse sides of the same intellectual phenomenon. The profound sense of change, movement, and development as constitutive of reality implied that the forms and words men use to apprehend and speak of what is "real" or "ultimate" or "true" are themselves fluid, partial, symbolic.[13]

Arnold's interpretation of the Bible and Christianity is a significant nineteenth-century theological expression of this dramatic "paradigm shift" we now take for granted.

I will limit my account of Arnold's theological reconstruction to *Literature and Dogma*, his most influential book on religion and his own favorite among his books. Upon its publication in 1873 it called forth a barrage of criticism both from orthodox divines on the right and from secular agnostics on the left--so much so, in fact, that Arnold immediately wrote another book, *God and the Bible* (1875), to respond to the criticisms and elaborate some of his arguments.

Literature and Dogma begins with a proposal that breathes the empirical spirit of the new age of "evolution and agnosticism": ". . .whatever is to stand must rest on something which is verifiable, not unverifiable."[14] The Bible and the Christian faith will engage the hearts and minds of people shaped by the modern *Zeitgeist*, says Arnold, only if they can test their claims in experience. The church's message increasingly strikes deaf ears because it is based on assumption, speculation, and not on what people can verify for themselves. Arnold takes up the task of giving the Bible and thereby the Christian faith "a real experimental basis,"[15] over against the ungrounded speculations presented as eternal facts of faith by orthodox theology.

Arnold finds the verifiable basis for religion in morality: "Now *morality* represents for everybody a thoroughly definite and ascertained idea:--the idea of human conduct regulated in a certain manner."[16] The purpose of religion is morality, conduct; and conduct, Arnold says in an oft-repeated phrase, is "three-

---

[13]Pp. 47-48.

[14]*Literature and Dogma: An Essay Towards a Better Apprehension of the Bible* (New York: AMS Press, 1970), ix.

[15]P. xi.

[16]P. 10.

fourths of life."17 Religion, in fact, "means simply either a binding to righteousness, or else a serious attending to righteousness and dwelling upon it."18 The difference between morality and religion, then, is one of degree, not of kind; but it is this difference that brings us to the heart of the matter. "Religion," he states, "is ethics heightened, enkindled, lit up by feeling; the passage from morality to religion is made, when to morality is applied emotion. And the true meaning of religion is thus not simply *morality*, but"--now comes the notorious part--"*morality touched by emotion.*"19 Of course, for Arnold the poet and man of letters "emotion" is not partial and sentimentalistic, but that depth and range of feeling that is the very well-spring of human thought and activity--what ancient Israel called "the heart."

Arnold's main task in *Literature and Dogma* was to develop the implications of this "moral-experiential" view of religion for understanding the Bible. The character of the biblical language was the crucial point at issue between Arnold and the orthodox theologians. "To understand that the language of the Bible is fluid, passing, and literary, not rigid, fixed, and scientific, is the first step towards a right understanding of the Bible."20 When Arnold talks about theology's treating biblical language as if it were "scientific," he is referring to the tendency of classical theological reflection to use the Bible as a sort of divine handbook of objective and harmonious assertions about God, humanity, and the universe. Theologians, Arnold charges, have taken what is essentially poetry, the imaginative outpouring of the human heart, and interpreted it as if it were a system of propositions about realities to which humans do not otherwise have access. But this violates the original and authentic function of biblical language; it forces it into an alien mould. To put it in contemporary linguistic-analytical terms, traditional theology has failed to recognize the way biblical language actually functioned for the people who used it.

Central to Arnold's discussion of biblical language is his analysis of the word "God," which more than any other feature of his "revisioning" reveals his religious liberalism and the metaphysically agnostic spirit it manifests. People use

17P. 13.
18P. 17.
19P. 18.
20P. xiii.

the word "God," he says, "as if it stood for a perfectly definite and ascertained idea, from which we might, without more ado, extract propositions and draw inferences."[21] But that is not how the biblical writers themselves use the word: "The language of the Bible. . .is literary, not scientific language; language *thrown out* at an object of consciousness not fully grasped, which inspired emotion."[22]

I want to emphasize Arnold's phrase "object of consciousness," because his view of God has often been taken as a form of theological reductionism or subjectivism. For Arnold language about God is poetic, but poetry is not merely subjective and non-referential but rather an essential way in which the human mind grasps and symbolizes the real. Hence "God-talk" refers to something other than human imaginings and projections. One of the verifiable facts of moral experience, according to Arnold, is "the very great part in righteousness which belongs, we may say, to *not ourselves*."[23] Moral life is in large part our human response to dynamic factors in our non-human environment and the inner "otherness" experienced in conscience which Arnold gathers up under the name "the Eternal," his rendering of the sense of the Hebrew name for God, Yahweh. The "not ourselves" of our human moral situation is an aspect of the mysterious encompassing reality which ancient Israel called "the Eternal." This "not ourselves" is the authentic referent of biblical language; although the referring, born out of the moral life by feeling and imagination, is "thrown out. . .at an object of consciousness not fully grasped" rather than comprehendingly asserted.

Arnold believes that the peculiar genius of ancient Israel lay in its clear insight into the moral character of religion and its corresponding "ontological" reticence. "They had dwelt upon the thought of conduct and right and wrong, till the *not ourselves* which is in us and around us, became to them adorable eminently and altogether as *a power which makes for righteousness*."[24] Israel at its best, in Moses and the prophetic tradition, kept its apprehension of God focussed on God's moral power in human life. They did not speculate vainly and "scientifically" about the nature of God, as did such modern churchmen as the Bishop of Gloucester who insisted on the necessity of holding correct opinions on the persons of the Trinity.

---

[21]P. 10.
[22]P. 36.
[23]P. 24.
[24]P. 28.

24

"The spirit and tongue of Israel kept a propriety, a reserve, a sense of the inadequacy of language in conveying man's ideas of God, which contrast strongly with the licence of affirmation in our Western theology. . . .Israel keeps to the language of poetry and does not essay the language of science."[25] Later Arnold asks, "is this reservedness of affirmation about God less worthy of him, than the astounding particularity and licence of affirmation of our dogmatists, as if he were a man in the next street?"[26]

God, then, is for Arnold "God for us," a transcendent power in our midst and within us about whom we speak haltingly and with the evocative language of poetry. What God is intrinsically is utterly beyond our experience or our grasp, and to erect the Christian theological system on the basis of speculation and specification regarding the inner nature of God is idolatry of the worst sort. In a chapter of *God and the Bible* entitled "The God of Metaphysics" Arnold elaborates on his anti-metaphysical approach to the problem of God. Engaging in a lengthy etymological analysis, he concludes that all talk of "being" is problematic in the extreme, and he reiterates his rejection of the standard theological affirmation that God is the supreme Person. To say that God must either be regarded as a person or reduced to the level of a thing, Arnold persuasively argues in a manner now familiar to us in theology, is a false alternative.[27]

Jesus' uniqueness is that in word and deed he recovered, intensified, and internalized Israel's grasp of righteousness as the essence of religion. Through his "method," inwardness, and his "secret," that the key to life is dying to self, Jesus is the highest and fullest expression of the reality of the "not ourselves" and of what human life can be. For Arnold the symbol of the kingdom of God is at the center of the gospel, which he takes to be the establishment of the rule of the "higher righteousness" in human life.

With views such as these Arnold clearly stands at the center of the liberal Protestant tradition in theology. As Livingston writes:

Arnold stands unmistakably in the tradition of modern Protestant

---

[25]P. 34.
[26]P. 53.
[27]*God and the Bible: A Sequel to "Literature and Dogma,"* R. H. Super, ed., *The Complete Prose Works of Matthew Arnold*, vol. VII (Ann Arbor: University of Michigan Press, 1970), 173-202.

liberalism with its roots both in Kant's metaphysical skepticism and his effort to establish religious belief on moral experience, as well as in Schleiermacher's experiential grounding of theology in religious feelings and the affections. The keys to this liberal tradition are *the experiential and the moral foundations of religious belief.*[28]

Arnold's closest affinities are with the Ritschlian liberals. Interestingly, he had read Schleiermacher but never read Ritschl. But, as Livingston says, "The parallels [with the Ritschlians] are striking."

> . . .Arnold shares with the Ritschlians an abhorrence of metaphysics and speculative theology; the rejection of ecclesiastical dogma as normative for faith; a practical, moral conception of religion and thus a sharp contrast between religious and scientific knowledge; the restriction of theological knowledge to the contents or effects of God's action on the moral consciousness and affections; the perception of Jesus' life and message as the normative revelation of the Christian "idea" or gospel; and the use of the kingdom of God as the regulative principle of the Christian community and its moral activity.[29]

Livingston goes on to point out the important ways in which, as an Anglican with a strong "catholic" sense of tradition, Arnold differs from Ritschlian Protestants and is closer to the Catholic Modernists. But it is clear that in the hermeneutical and theological approach that lies at the heart of his work he stands in the liberal Protestant tradition.

3. Skeptics and liberals: uneasy comrades

Arnold's theological reconstruction--of which I have presented only the barest outline--makes clear his mediating position between the reigning theology on the one hand and scientific skepticism on the other. Like many mediators, he was appreciated by neither side. He agreed with the scientific temper of the age that belief must be experientially grounded, verifiable, and non-metaphysical, but he interpreted this much more broadly than, say, Huxley or Leslie Stephen did, with his talk about the cognitive realism of poetry and the "not ourselves" in moral experience. As a man who not only drew deeply upon the Christian tradition in his

---

[28]*Matthew Arnold and Christianity,* 178.
[29]P. 180.

religious life but also had a profound sense of cultural continuity, Arnold deplored a Christian establishment that was busily alienating the best minds in Britain; but he likewise rejected the secular substitutes as impoverishments of the human spirit. Livingston nicely summarizes his views on this point:

> Arnold considered the loss of the Bible's influence on the nation as tragic, for he viewed the secular alternatives of Spencer, Comte, Bradlaugh, and Leslie Stephen as either fatuous nonsense or unctuous truism when compared with the sublimity and the morally transforming power of the biblical literature. What Arnold called for was a reading of the Bible anew in its original, natural light. So read, the Bible, he believed, would no longer be viewed as "prescientific error" but as that which must remain as the indispensable complement to our scientific work--without which our lives would become selfish and narrow, lacking all spiritual grace and vision.[30]

The issue here between Arnold and the secular agnostics can be seen at one level as an early expression of the debate between the classical empiricism represented by Hume and the more holistic "radical empiricism" of, say, William James, as Livingston perceptively observes.[31]

Among the secular agnostics of Victorian Britain Huxley was certainly one who could appreciate the persuasiveness of and sympathize with Arnold's mediating efforts. But the objections of other skeptical critics of *Literature and Dogma* such as the former Anglican priest Leslie Stephen and the Comtean positivist Frederic Harrison were twofold. One was the standard secular criticism of liberal attempts at theological reconstruction that they are a reduction of Christianity to a kind of "depth humanism" that essentially abandons the historic faith. The other was a conviction that the enterprise was hopelessly quixotic, the attempt to breathe new life into a moribund tradition when what was needed was a new foundation of religion and morality for a scientific age.

This conversation between the liberal Christian and the secular humanist who share the agnostic spirit has been an ongoing one down to the present day. For reasons some of which I have explored in this essay, the religious liberal and

---

[30]P. 45.

[31]Pp. 99-102. See Nancy Frankenberry, *Religion and Radical Empiricism* (Albany: SUNY Press, 1987), for a history of modern empiricism and the chief differences between classical and radical forms of empiricism.

the interested skeptic have tended to see in each other simultaneously a close kinship and the most telling critique of their respective positions.

By temperament, education, life choices, and intellectual evaluations, Huxley and Arnold came down on opposite sides of the liberal fence in Victorian Britain. But they shared that agnostic frame of mind regarding the authority of experience and our ignorance of what lies beyond it that made them sensitive to the views and concerns of the other. While they debated the proper role of the sciences in a liberal education,[32] Huxley was a man of considerable humanistic learning and culture and Arnold was no ignoramus about science. We have seen that Huxley appreciated the efforts of liberal theologians, urged them to make their case as strongly as possible, and considered that they had essentially accepted the "agnostic principle." Arnold, for his part, was relentless and caustic in his all-out attack on orthodox theology in a way that made Huxley rejoice. Arnold's insistence that the biblical writings be read as literature and interpreted from the standpoint of broad acquaintance with "the best that has been thought and said in the world" was at least in principle quite congenial to Huxley. Interestingly, both favored the retention of instruction in the Bible in the schools, and both believed it should be taught by trained teachers and not by clerics.

A study of Arnold and Huxley, I believe, furnishes us a significant paradigm of both the close relationship and the interesting differences between liberal Christians and sympathetic skeptics that have been an important feature of critical religious thought over the past century. It is a dialogue grounded in a shared agnostic spirit that has expressed itself in a rich variety of ways in the "borderlands" between belief and unbelief.

---

[32]See, e.g., Huxley's "Science and Culture" in *Selections from the Essays*, 41-45; and Arnold's "Literature and Science" in *Poetry and Criticism of Matthew Arnold*, edited and with an introduction and notes by A. Dwight Culler (Boston: Houghton Mifflin, 1961), 381-396.

Chapter 3

Humane Vision: Theological Norm and Dialogical Platform

All our primary orientations to reality, whether "religious" or "secular," are ways of interpreting the world and the human situation for which reasons are necessary but never entirely sufficient--although that does not entail that none are more reasoned and reasonable than others. All our visionings and re-visionings of life are shaped and limited by our cultural context--although that does not mean that they do not also in part transcend that context and contain universal dimensions. By their very nature, our various world-interpretations are formed out of a complex interplay of individual experience, imagination, reason, and feeling--although that does not mean that we cannot and should not become self-critical and self-corrective regarding these several elements and their roles.

Gods, whatever else they are, function as the imaginative centers or focal ideals of many people's visionings of life. As the key symbols in comprehensive life-interpretations, gods fulfill aesthetic, cognitive, and moral as well as religious needs. When they are taken seriously, gods inspire and energize persons both for good and for ill.

Although I have stated and summarized them in my own way, the above are standard observations which can be found in the anthropological, sociological, psychological, philosophical, and theological literature of our time. They provide, I believe, a common meeting-ground between theists and non-theists by reminding us of (1) the existential character and contextual limitations of all our primary interpretations of the world, and (2) the actual role that belief in God plays in theistic interpretations of the world. My observations also suggest to me a functional criterion by which to evaluate and link together both theistic and non-theistic visions of life: the extent to which they express what I call a *humane vision* of the world.

I have been using the terms "vision" or "visioning" of life to refer to persons' overall interpretations of or perspectives on reality. Visions of life may of course be inchoate or highly reflective, naive or critical, crude or sophisticated, dishevelled or coherent. As I have indicated, life-visions embody elements of cultural context, individual experience, feeling, imagination, and reason. They also clearly involve both contemplation and action, knowledge and practice.

In defining humane vision I adopt and adapt both standard meanings of the term "humane": (1) compassionately concerned for human beings; and (2) committed to those values which most fully "civilize" or enrich human life. Compassionate concern embodies sympathy for and sensitivity toward human beings in both their bondages and their possibilities. It expresses itself practically in the active affirmation of justice, freedom, and community. Those values which most fully "refine" or "humanize" human life include truthfulness and the self-critical search for truth, the celebration of beauty and the imagination, and the common pursuit of the good society as one in which human suffering is alleviated and human diversity and possibility are supported. Especially in the context of contemporary thought and life another aspect of humane vision should also be made explicit: its recognition of the unity and interdependence of all life. Fully appreciating that to be human is never an abstraction but always to be a unique person in a particular cultural and social context, humane visions of life at the same time constantly seek to move us beyond the tribalism that so stubbornly continues to dominate our most fundamental ways of interpreting and acting in the world into a universal vision of humankind. Humane visions are furthermore at their fullest ecological, situating the human sphere within the context of and inextricably bound up with our fellow creatures in a delicate and vital web of interdependence.

Humane visions of life exist in both theistic and non-theistic versions. Humane vision explicitly informs non-theistic varieties of liberal humanism, as in the thought and life of figures such as George Eliot, Charlotte Perkins Gilman,

John Dewey, and Albert Camus. But humane vision is also the motive force and operative framework--sometimes explicit but often implicit--of liberal varieties of Jewish and Christian theism. I want to propose that the implicit needs to be made fully explicit in theological hermeneutics, and that one result will be to make even clearer the elements common to liberal theisms and humanisms.[1] But my claim and proposal need some elaboration at this point.

1. Theological norm

Albeit in a great variety of ways, Jews and Christians look to their scriptures as a foundationally authoritative source for their respective interpretations of reality. Many would acknowledge at the same time that the scriptural witness to God, the world, human beings, and values is a decidedly "mixed bag," and would be at pains to point out that the scriptures must be interpreted with sensibility and humanity and with an appropriately humble sense of the fallibility of scripture itself and all our interpretations of scripture.

But reflective Jews and Christians who interpret the biblical sources expansively and humanely are doing more than practicing knowledgeable and balanced exegesis. Although often not every explicitly or consciously, they are inspired by a vision of the divine and the human which has its origins in scripture but its criteria in their own highest values--in what I have called humane vision. In their theological reflection they are engaged in a creative dialectical movement back and forth between two poles: on the one side the biblical literature as a foundational source of their world-perspective and a continuing source of renewal and insight; and on the other a universal normative vision of the *summum bonum* shaped by other sources as well, developed over many centuries, and expressed concretely in the cultural situation of their day.

Examples of what I am talking about abound in modern Jewish and Christian thought. To mention only some: Fredrich Schleiermacher and the other nineteenth-century German liberal Protestant thinkers, William Ellery Channing and Unitarianism, Walter Rauschenbusch and the Social Gospel movement, Leo Baeck and the Reform Jewish theological tradition. In contemporary Christian thought the

---

[1]I began wrestling with this issue in a more internally theological way in a 1973 book, *Borderland Christianity: Critical Reason and the Christian Vision of Love* (Nashville: Abingdon Press).

liberation theologies are representative, with their frank appeal to the humane values derived from black experience, women's experience, or the experience of Third World poor as criteria for interpreting the Bible. The following statement by the feminist liberation theologian Rosemary Ruether illustrates what I mean:

> The equality of women, as one of the touchstones for understanding our faithfulness to the vision, is now set forth as one of the norms for criticizing the tradition and discovering its best expressions. This will create a radical reappraisal of Jewish and Christian traditions, since much that has been regarded as marginal, and even heretical, must now be seen as an effort to hold onto an authentic tradition of women's equality. Much of the tradition regarded as mainstream must be seen as deficient in this regard. We underestimate the radical intent of women's studies in religion if we do not recognize that it aims at nothing less than a radical reconstruction of the normative tradition.[2]

Similarly, Tom Driver in his book *Christ in a Changing World: Toward an Ethical Christology*[3] explicitly develops a christology using as a hermeneutical norm contemporary liberal socioethical values. In the Jewish tradition, Eugene Borowitz has long been the chief American exponent of a liberal Jewish theology which fully affirms the modern moral norm of personal autonomy in dialectical balance with Jewish tradition.[4] What we typically find, however, is that many contemporary liberal theologians continue to "hedge their bets" methodologically, in two ways: (1) by failing to be crystal clear about what their hermeneutical presuppositions really are; and (2) by justifying their interpretation as "what the Bible *really* means." The latter appeal shows up even in the works of theologians such as Ruether and Driver. What I wrote in 1973 on this issue still seems to me to be accurate as a characterization of much contemporary Christian thought; the material quoted is from *Borderland Christianity*:

> . . ."modern" theologians have seemed reverently to bend the knee before the absoluteness and all-sufficiency of the biblical Christ, while in fact and with varying degrees of awareness they

---

[2]Ruether, *Disputed Questions: On Being a Christian* (Nashville: Abingdon Press, 1982), 125.

[3](New York: Crossroad, 1981).

[4]See, e.g., his *A New Jewish Theology in the Making* (Philadelphia: Westminster, 1968).

have appealed, rather than to the biblical Christ himself, to a higher norm by which they interpret and evaluate all his uncomfortable and limiting aspects.[5]

The refreshingly free hand with which the older liberal Protestant thinkers interpreted Christianity, the Niebuhr brothers' stimulating reflections on the relations between Christianity and culture, Bonhoeffer's "nonreligious interpretation," the volumes that continue to pour forth about Christianity and technology, environment, race, sex, politics, revolution--all this reads quite coherently as attempts to apply the logic of. . .[what I have called] "agapeic vision" to modern life, but rather dubiously and tortuously as christocentric biblical interpretation.[6]

. . .recent theological movements [have] uncovered highly fruitful insights at the Christian source into decisive phenomena of our time. But is it necessary to insist, with one-sided exegesis and other contortions, that this is what the Bible and Jesus "really" mean?. . .If there are, in the remembered and interpreted Jesus of the new Testament, creative implications for modern thought and perspectival criteria which aid in illuminating and assessing our age, that represents an important theological contribution to our knowledge and our attitudes. . . .If insights are believed to be consistent with the Christian vision of divine love as it has unfolded down to this point in history, they can stand on that basis; they do not need the additional sanction and authority of "what Jesus really meant to say or do.". . .But there is a kind of unexamined tradition about "what Christian theology is obligated to be," in which everyone by gentleman's agreement continues to follow certain rules about being "biblical" and "christocentric" without admitting that this is neither necessary, desireable, nor what really goes on in their reflections.[7]

Historical-critical knowledge of the biblical sources has of course been an important factor in rendering theological appeals to biblical norms highly problematic. At the same time, the biblical roots of humane vision in its Jewish and Christian forms are not hard to identify although they are richly diverse in their expressions. They are those strands in the Hebrew Bible and the Apostolic Writings which attest that the abysmal Mystery with which humans have to do is characterized by active, unconditional, "steadfast love" for humans and the world.

---

[5]P. 38.
[6]P. 40.
[7]Pp. 71-72.

Bound up with that audacious vision of reality are the affirmations of the goodness of the world as the ongoing creation of that love, our human involvement in and responsibility for the world as dialogical partners with the divine, and the worth of human persons as conscious creaturely subjects of that creative and redemptive love. At the biblical roots of humane vision are also to be found penetrating insights into the mysterious bondage of the human condition and our ultimate dependence upon grace. At the same time there are the clear demands laid upon human beings finitely to imitate the love of God in compassion and justice among persons and in human communities as the very law of human life. And animating faithful human action in the world is the eschatological vision of the kingdom of God as future promise and present ideal.

But these foundational elements of humane vision--as biblical scholarship has so emphatically driven home--were inevitably expressed in and limited by the ancient Near Eastern cultural forms which were their human context. They have undergone extensive development, elaboration, and reinterpretation in both the Jewish and the Christian traditions under changing historical and cultural circumstances. No theologian who expects to be taken seriously believes that Jewish and Christian belief and thought today either are or can possibly be simply a matter of repeating the Bible or pretending that we can stand where ancient Israel and the early Christian community stood. We must deal with cultural realities and problems that the biblical writers could neither know nor anticipate. Our knowledge of the world and ourselves and our values have many sources other than the biblical literature.

The hermeneutical art in theology and theological ethics is the creative working out of appropriate methods for relating the biblical foundations to the issues and the knowledge of an ever-changing and dramatically changed world, in the context of a vision of the most fully humane values of which are capable. It is a dialogical task which, because of the historical character of human existence, must of course be always renewed and always unfinished. What I am proposing is that the idea of humane vision be acknowledged as a conscious criterion and framework for the Jewish and Christian hermeneutical task. As I have indicated, I think it is clear that as a matter of fact it already functions as the real context for liberal forms of Jewish and Christian reflection, but usually tacitly, somewhat obscurely, and at times even a bit disingenuously.

I want to focus now on the center of theological reflection, the idea of God, because I believe that the venerable theological quest for *conceptual adequacy* in the idea of God provides theological justification for the appeal to humane vision. Anselm's succinct formal definition of God as "a being than which nothing more perfect can be conceived" has with good reason been viewed as articulating a primary motive in the historic Western discussion of the divine attributes. We must as a matter of theological priority continue to be guided by the question: How are we most adequately to symbolize and conceptualize--as much as our human grasp will allow--what we believe to be truly ultimate in being and value?

The demand for conceptual adequacy in the idea of God thus brings sharply into focus the rationale for humane vision as theological presupposition and criterion. In attempting to conceive of what is for us truly "greatest" in being and value, we are rationally obliged to begin with the highest values we are capable of envisioning in the context of the best knowledge we have. For Jews and Christians such reflection will surely include the biblical foundations as a core element, but hardly as either a conclusive or an inclusive word.

The great biblical ideas and images are inexhaustibly rich primary metaphors pointing beyond their particular historical-cultural embodiments. Down through the centuries of the Common Era they have been successively reinterpreted with new insight by the Jewish and Christian theological traditions in the light of new historical circumstances and new sources of knowledge. Intimately bound up with this history of biblical hermeneutics are of course dramatic material changes in the idea of the perfection of God. We do well to recall that once upon a time most Christians believed that the One who is goodness and justice itself commanded the merciless annihilation of enemies, inquisitions against heretics, crusades against Muslim "infidels," persecution of Jews and "witches," and the subjugation of women. If we now find such things abhorrent and simply incompatible with "the teaching of the Bible," it is because we have learned to read the Bible differently. Our notions of an adequate God have changed because our visions of life have changed, under the impact of the developments in empirical knowledge, the transformations in our perceptions of moral values, and the course of human events.

My proposal as it pertains to the idea of God should by now be unsurprising: It is that theological reflection on God should be consciously guided by a biblically-informed humane vision and not by the biblical writings. This seems to me clearly to be what liberal Jewish and Christian theologians already do. Again, I am simply urging that this salutary methodological presupposition and practice be affirmed quite explicitly as a hermeneutical model. Conscious adoption of this practicing norm means that liberal forms of theism will of course continue to be quite as pluralistic as they have been. Humane vision as a criterion for God-talk by no means yields uniformity: not only do people differ in their articulation of humane vision, but they can also move in various directions from the known to the less known and still remain consistent. Feminist theologians--Jewish, Christian, and neo-pagan--are doing some of the most creative and provocative rethinking of the idea of God today, in the context of their highest affirmations of value; not at all unrelated are other varied approaches such as we find in process theologies and empirical theologies.

At the same time, a shared vision of life that is informed by compassion for human beings and a commitment to those values which most fully "humanize" human life characteristically expresses itself in views of God which reject or reinterpret those traditional images and attributes of God bound up with absolute power and rule. This is a consistent theme in contemporary liberal Jewish and Christian thought, from the "death of God" theologians who radically articulated it in the sixties to feminist and process theologians; and its roots can be traced to philosophical and theological currents of the nineteenth century. Put in another way, the "perfection" or "ultimacy" to be ascribed to God has undergone in modern theology a striking redefinition in the light largely of considerations which I have incorporated into the term "humane vision."

2. Dialogical platform

Since humane vision explicitly informs non-theistic varieties of liberal humanism and functionally animates liberal forms of theism, they clearly share essential elements of a common vision. This statement will of course hardly come as news to those in the Unitarian Universalist tradition or to participants in liberal humanism and liberal theism generally. Rosemary Ruether and Tom Driver have much more in common with Michael Harrington than they do with Jerry Falwell. The "dialogical platform" between liberal humanisms and theisms provided by their common commitment to humane vision has long existed and been recognized. My chief purpose here has been to challenge liberal forms of theology to be fully conscious and consistent about their hermeneutical agenda, and thereby to realize even more clearly the extent to which they share a common vision with liberal humanisms.

If we can identify liberal theisms and humanisms alike by their commitment to humane vision, wherein do they differ? Perhaps a useful way to understand the difference is to say that non-theistic humanisms are more skeptical about the ontological status of the humane values they affirm. Liberal theists are characteristically tentative, undogmatic, and open-ended about their theistic affirmations. But their faith typically consists in their belief, for whatever reasons they may variously adduce, that the values of truth, beauty, and goodness are in some way grounded in God or what is taken to be ontologically ultimate. For most liberal theists this assures the imperishability of such values and thus the ontological worthwhileness of pursuing them in a frightfully ambiguous and ever-changing world.

But a liberal theistic faith may be quite confident or exceedingly tenuous. It may express itself in the elaborated reasoning of process theology or as a kind of anguished existentialist "leap." Liberal theisms range theologically over a spectrum which at one end shades off into agnosticism. Not infrequently the liberal theist is a person who lives in the "borderlands" between theism and humanism: one might say, not entirely facetiously, a believer on Mondays, Wednesdays, Fridays, and Sundays, and an agnostic on Tuesdays, Thursdays, and Saturdays. Over the years I have become increasingly impressed by the complexity and fluidity of reflective persons' faith or world-orientation. At least among the liberal theists I know and know of, to say that this or that individual is a "believer" as opposed to a "skeptic," a "Christian" in contrast to a "non-Christian," is to oversimplify and pigeonhole somewhat.

As I said at the beginning of this essay, our various orientations to life, besides being culturally shaped, express a complex interplay of individual experience, imagination, reason, and feeling. We dearly love to categorize persons and their beliefs as well as everything else under the sun, and thereby miss their full, many-sided, and often elusive reality. Given the very nature of *liberal* theisms and humanisms, it seems to me that there is a danger of overstating or overdefining their differences. I said that generally speaking the liberal humanist is more skeptical than the liberal theist about the ontological status of the values they both affirm. But liberal theism may and typically does involve a considerable measure of skepticism, while the liberal humanist is quite capable of being humbly open-minded about the possibility that there are more things in heaven and earth than are dreamt of in his or her philosophy. If we further look at theistic affirmation functionally, as I suggested at the outset, God for the liberal theist serves as the imaginative center of focal ideal of her or his humane vision, while other alternatives may fulfill the same function for the liberal humanist.

It is a common commitment to a humane vision of life which liberal theisms and humanisms clearly share; and that commitment to compassion for human beings and to those values which grace and ennoble and expand human life is what urgently matters. Serious and wondering exploration of the limits and possibilities of our knowledge and of the nature of reality is precisely one of those humane values, and liberal humanists and theists engage and ought to engage together in that important and never-finished quest. But the embodiment of humane vision in the world cannot wait upon the resolution of the problem of God: too many persons cry out for help, too many issues hang in the balance. As Sartre famously observed, the fact of our responsibility remains whether or not God exists.

3. A dialogical invitation and challenge

My remarks at the end of the preceding section bring me, in this final portion of my essay, to a consideration of the late Michael Harrington's substantial and provocative book, *The Politics at God's Funeral: The Spiritual Crisis of Western Civilization.*[8] The thesis of the book is that "the God of the Judeo-Christian west is in his death agony and that is one of the most significant political events of this incredible age." (11) The God whose decline and death Harrington traces is not God as continuing object of personal faith for many people, but God as powerful integrative symbol of Western civilization: the God who has functioned as "the legitimation of established power and sometimes of revolt against it; the transcendent symbol of the common consciousness of an existing community; the foundation of all other values; the organizing principle of a system of the

---

[8](N.Y.: Penguin, 1983). Quotations from the book will be followed simply by the page numbers.

authoritative allocation of social roles (the God of Western feudalism) or the motivating and ethical principle of a system of individual mobility (the God of Western capitalism); the guarantor of personal, ethnic and national identity; a philosopher for the non-philosophers, including the illiterate." (7-8) Beginning with the Enlightenment, Harrington devotes most of the book to a highly informed and perceptive interpretation of the fate of the Judaeo-Christian God in the modern world. An important strength of the book, and one we would expect from Harrington, is his concern always to show the mutually influencing relationship among the intellectual, the religious, the social, and the political.

Thus Harrington's main thesis, and the impressive intellectual-historical analysis with which he argues for it. A subsidiary thesis of the book is one which issues in a call to dialogue and action. Raised a Roman Catholic, Harrington (borrowing a phrase from Simmel) called himself a "religious nature without religion," an atheist who was also a prominent and active democratic Marxist and national co-chair of the Democratic Socialists of America. His subsidiary thesis is bound up with his main thesis: The spiritual crisis of the late twentieth century--the dying of the God of Western civilization--is essentially bound up with our societal and political crises, and it is serious atheists and serious believers who grasp what is going on and who thus must make common cause in the articulation and defense of common moral values against the practicing, humanly destructive nihilisms of our time. In the remainder of my paper I want to expound Harrington's elaboration of his subsidiary thesis in the final chapter of the book, "Prolegomena to a Political Morality."

The question with which the concluding chapter opens and which it tries to answer is this: "Can Western society create transcendental common values in its everyday experience? Values which are not based upon--yet not counterposed to-- the supernatural?" (197) Harrington never makes precisely clear what he means by using the term "transcendental," although it is not difficult to make out from his discussion that he intends by it to emphasize that the values of which he speaks are of a universal and enduring sort rather than particularistic and ephemeral. The closest he comes to a kind of "definition" of transcendental values is in his references to a speech the Neo-Thomist philosopher Jacques Maritain made at a UNESCO conference in 1947, when he responded to the phenomenon of ideological "Babelism" in the modern world:

There could be, Maritain rightly commented, no consensus
on basic philosophic issues and world views. That was the
problem, not the solution. But there could be a coming together on
"common practical notions," "not in the affirmation of the same
conception of the world, man and knowledge but in the affirmation
of the same set of convictions concerning action." If this was not an
ideological agreement, it was something more than a joint program
for action since it involved "a sort of common residue, a sort of
unwritten common law, at the point of practical convergence of
extremely different theoretical ideologies and spiritual traditions."
This, Maritain rightly concluded, was a development of "major
importance." (203-204)

Thus "transcendental values" are generally equivalent to what the Western
philosophical and theological traditions have referred to with such concepts as
natural law, the *consensus gentium*, or "common notions": basic moral values
which seem sooner or later to be generally affirmed by human beings in their
common life together, however variously embodied and admixed with markedly
different cultural customs and traditions. Harrington clearly does not want to hang
any metaphysical baggage on the notion, and his consistent talk about humans
"creating" (and failing to create) such values indicates that for him such values
emerge out of the conditions of human life and a common human intentionality
rather than reflecting the mind of God or a "transcendent" moral order. What I have
called humane vision is an articulation of what Harrington calls transcendental
values, and my own description is neutral with regard to their ontological
foundations.

The question with which Harrington begins his "Prolegomena" is central
and urgent to our time, he believes, because of the conclusion he has drawn from
his intellectual-historical analysis of the dying of the Judaeo-Christian God as the
integrating symbol of Western values. Harrington believes that Nietzsche was
correct in thinking that

the death of God has . . . pointed toward the death of all the higher
values. For hundreds of years those values were, consciously or
not, rooted in the assumption of an absolute order in the universe,
guaranteed by God. When God and morality and religion were
relativized by the new scientific, historical, sociological and
anthropological consciousness of the nineteenth century, a good part
of traditional Western culture was undermined. And when, in the

twentieth century, it became increasingly difficult to believe in optimistic theories of liberal or social progress, the crisis became all the more severe. I do not think that it is an overgeneralization of the evidence presented in this book to say that masses of people in the West no longer know what they believe. (201-202)

Harrington sums up his analysis and issues his challenge in this way: "there is no way back--or forward--to a religious integration of society on the model of Judeo-Christianity in any of its manifestations. But there is a need for the transcendental. That is why the conflict between religious and atheistic humanism must now be ended." (202)

Dismissing the old conflicts between Christianity and an anticlerical atheism as completely *passé* and irrelevant, Harrington begins to articulate his appeal for a common cause by saying that "atheist and agnostic humanists should be as appalled by *de facto* atheism in late capitalist society as should people of religious faith. It is a thoughtless, normless, selfish, hedonistic individualism." (202-203) He goes on to state his common agenda: ". . . serious atheists and agnostics now share a common cause with serious believers: a concern for values as such, for a vision of individual and social meaningfulness which goes beyond the latest consumer or cultural fad." (203) During this time of the death of the God of the Western religious tradition, the "absence of serious thought about the human condition" is the common enemy of both theistic and non-theistic humanism.

Harrington attempts to provide at least a kind of blueprint for practical forms of cooperation, describing the infusion of "new" Catholic socialists into the secular socialist movement in France after World War II. Through the influence of the communitarian tradition from Catholicism, the refurbished French socialism abandoned the old centralized, collectivized models for one that was "worker-managed, decentralized, communitarian"--a shift which can now be seen in socialist parties throughout Western Europe. "That French experience," Harrington writes,

> might even serve as a model for the consensus being proposed here.
> . . . it meant that both the traditional socialists and the new socialists
> changed themselves, that in the process of uniting they discovered
> (rediscovered) new (old) values. I am suggesting something like
> that as a political-spiritual project for all of Western society. It is not
> that the religious people are being offered a gracious opportunity to
> surrender all of their principles. Rather, they are being urged to
> bring those of their religious principles which are relevant to a

secular politics into that politics, to enrich it and broaden it. (206)

Part of the uniquely religious contribution, Harrington believes, lies precisely in the communitarian experience and reflection of the theistic traditions. He notes that the Catholic Church, speaking out of a long theological tradition of affirming human dignity in genuinely human community, has in its social teaching been consistently critical of both socialism and capitalism for their collectivistic and individualistic distortions which depersonalize and exploit.

Harrington proposes and briefly sketches four common "transcendentals" as the foundation of the new consensus between serious humanists and theists, "value judgments . . . which can be arrived at within the framework of practically every serious Western tradition, secular as well as religious" (209): (1) the legitimacy of laws and political structures as grounded only upon the effective *participation* of the members of the society in their formulation; (2) *community* as the experiential basis for affirming common values; (3) an expansion of *moral motivation* based upon concrete human solidarity; and (4) the *universalizability* or global relevance of these values forged out of modern Western experience. Harrington grants that these values have become platitudes or clichés in Western thought and life, maintaining that their familiarity is both a weakness and a strength: a weakness in that it is difficult to get people to take them seriously, a strength in that they clearly form a deep-rooted "common residue" for a new and active value consensus.

Not surprisingly, Harrington concludes his "Prolegomena" by offering a democratic socialism as the most viable practical embodiment of the new value consensus. Sharply critical of both Soviet socialism and Western capitalism for their elitism, authoritarianism, and anti-communitarianism, he proposes four principles of political policy and action which would incarnate the new value consensus: (1) the promotion of human community as a criterion for the effectiveness of any national economic plan, with a particular emphasis on achieving this at "the most immediate, intimate level of social life" (217); (2) the encouragement of moral incentives rather than economic incentives in motivating social behavior--reducing the "punishments of failure and the rewards of success" conceived in purely economic terms; (3) the extension of the democratic ideal of widespread participation both politically and economically; and (4) the formulation of national policy, so far as possible, in such a way as to help the most vulnerable members of the human family. In other books Harrington has spelled out in detail the implementation of such policies. He concludes the "Prolegomena" on this note:

> My practical point is that men and women of faith and anti-faith should, in the secular realm at least, stop fighting one another and begin to work together to introduce moral dimensions into economic and social debate and decision. That means that the structures of corporate "rationality" will have to be challenged in the name of a human rationality. We are emerging into a much more collective time, in each nation and even when anti-collective conservatives rule; and explicit values are becoming more socially important than they have been for four hundred years. (218)

The "new value consensus" proposed by Harrington as a platform for agreement and action between theists and humanists is clearly an articulation of humane vision. I have used it as a kind of "case study" for my essay, because I believe that Harrington's analysis of the crisis of values in the contemporary West and his appeal to "serious" believers and non-believers to come together on the basis of their common commitment to "transcendental values" should be considered very seriously, whatever criticisms we may have of certain of their details. Harrington develops his proposals entirely from out of a social-democratic context. One might legitimately consider that a somewhat limiting frame of reference, whether on theoretical grounds or for reasons of political feasibility in the U.S. But the humane values of community, democratic participation, moral incentives, and special concern for the most vulnerable members of society, are surely matters on which many theists and humanists of good will agree and concerning which they ought to and do speak out and act in concert.

I want in closing to call attention to a point on which I believe Harrington is not sufficiently explicit--one which is perhaps clarified by the proposals I have made in this essay. He speaks only of "serious" religious believers, without distinguishing further, meaning by "serious" those who affirm the sort of humane vision he sketches in the final chapter. At the same time, he has no use whatever for the fundamentalist right which in the 1980s became so visible in American politics. They apparently do not count as "serious," although in the ordinary sense of the term they can of course be very serious indeed. Harrington might have clarified things with some sort of notion such as I have suggested with the idea of humane vision. What he really means by "serious" theists and humanists is persons on both sides who share a primary commitment to humane vision. While my own discussion has limited itself to what I have broadly called "liberal" theists and humanists, there are clearly orthodox and conservative Christians and Jews who are actively motivated by humane vision. The crucial distinction is not between the theologically "liberal" and "conservative," but rather between those who are committed to some version of humane vision and those who are not.

In an ideologically pluralistic and largely secular world the values we share transmitted to us chiefly through the Jewish and Christian traditions are not the religious ones, although for many those values will continue to be grounded in religious practice and theological considerations. What theists and humanists share of the Judaeo-Christian heritage and those other sources of which it has been the main mediator is a spectrum of primarily moral values ranging from respect for persons to the unfettered search for truth. It is a rich and varied consensus on "transcendentals" upon which commonly to build. I have suggested the notion of humane vision as the most fully humane and humanizing expression of that consensus, and have argued that it is the real agenda for much contemporary theology as well as for non-theistic forms of humanism.

Chapter 4

The Future of American Liberal Religious Thought: A Critical Perspective

I take it as established that American liberal religious thought has exhibited great variety, existing in Christian, Jewish, and more broadly theistic and humanistic forms; and that in its multiform religious quest it is generally unified by a commitment to the reconciliation of religious faith with the perceived claims of reason and of something roughly called "modern culture." I also assume that one is not at liberty to say absolutely anything under the sun about the future: presumably the speculation that "liberal religious thought will become committed to irrationality" is in some analytical sense completely unwarranted, unless the speculator invests the term "irrationality" with dramatically new meaning. Responsible prediction will approach its task with the intellectual-moral virtues of humility and informed judgment. It will proceed cautiously with its inferences on the basis of solid knowledge of the past and present of the subject in question combined with a respectful openness to the fact that historical unfolding is marked more by surprise than by inevitabilities.

But I envision my own look at the American liberal religious future here in even more modest terms. I am much less interested in speculating on the future development and viability of liberal religious thought than I am in trying to discern what the future agenda of liberal religious grapplings with the issues of ultimate reality and meaning should contain. I assume--I trust not naively--that in the modern, irrevocably pluralistic West for the foreseeable future, liberal religious reflection will be represented in theological interchange. Nor am I chiefly interested in whether or not conservatives and fundamentalists are "taking over" American Christianity at least for the time being, or in what the membership statistics of the more liberal denominations and of Reform Judaism will be in the year 2000. Those are legitimate questions, but I am not the person to deal with them. My preoccupations and competencies are philosophical, theological, and intellectual-historical. Within that framework I feel myself to be on the surest footing if I confine myself to the effort to articulate, on the basis of contemporary knowledge and practice, those issues that I see as central to theological reflection for the proximate future. I consider them issues to which all religious thought should be attentive; but I present and discuss them in terms of their specific relations to liberal religion and to the American religio-cultural context within which I and most of my readers dwell.

I have subtitled my essay "A Critical Perspective." In posing an agenda for subsequent liberal religious thought in America, I am at the same time evaluating the liberal religious tradition. By my choice of theological themes and the ways I describe them, I am highlighting what I consider to be both strengths and weaknesses of that tradition and calling it to continued self-criticism and growth. My discussion in the remainder of this essay is intended to be both affirmation and correction, both challenge and critique.

In speaking of strengths and weaknesses in a phenomenon as historically and intellectually varied as American liberal religion, I must of course generalize and thereby run the considerable but necessary risk of over-generalizing. I can talk only of certain general tendencies, characteristics, or emphases, always keenly aware that not all liberal religious thinkers share such tendencies and that liberal religious thinkers have disagreed sharply among themselves. Historically, liberal religious thought in both America and Europe has undergone successive chastenings and revisions under the impact of new knowledge, rival theologies, and world events. No contemporary liberal feels bound by Friedrich Schleiermacher or Albrecht Ritschl, Walter Rauschenbusch or Shailer Mathews. Conceptually, there are important metaphysical, epistemological, and methodological differences--between say, a Paul Tillich and a Henry Nelson Wieman, between Christian and humanist liberals. I must beg my readers, in the pages that follow, to remember what I have just said, and I hope that I am not completely missing the mark in pointing up some of the general tendencies I discern in liberal religious thought:

Shielded, then, by the above qualifications, I make so bold as to list what I consider to be important tendencies or emphases in American liberal religious thought, most of which will figure in various ways in the agenda I want to propose for the liberal future:

--a preference for the languages of science, philosophy and ethics over the languages of myth and story;

--the assumption of scientific knowledge, in the broad sense of that term, as in one way or another paradigmatic or normative;

--following from the above, a significant interest in what might broadly be called "natural" or "philosophical" theology more than in "revealed" or "dogmatic" theology;

--allowing for all the ways in which this emphasis has historically been caricatured and misunderstood, nevertheless a theological focus on divine immanence more than on divine transcendence;

--again granting past misrepresentations, an anthropocentric more than a theocentric or even a cosmocentric perspective;

--although famously appealing to (human) "experience," a tendency to focus more on the cognitive and the conative than on the affective and irrational aspects of experience;

--despite the openness to sociological and psychological accounts of human behavior and to twentieth-century events, a larger stress on human freedom than on human bondage;

--in terms of the classical theological debate, an emphasis on "works" or human agency and activity more than on "grace" or human dependence and "giftedness";

--intimately linked with the above, a preoccupation with ethics and decision more than with contemplation and receptivity;

--a recognition that the personal has no meaning except in the context of and in interaction with the social;

--a thoroughgoing this-worldliness, often combined with a sitting very lightly to or even rejecting notions of "life after death."

The general theme of my proposed agenda for future directions in American liberal religious thought is a call for *wholeness* and *realism* in its pursuit of ultimate reality and meaning. That of course suggests that in some respects liberalism is lacking in those qualities; and in terms of some of the tendencies I have just described that is indeed my view. But if my challenge to liberal religion points to what I consider deficiencies, it also build upon and seeks to extend what I consider to be enduring virtues. It is precisely in terms of the central liberal commitments to *reason* and *experience*--that is, in terms of liberalism's own logic--that I highlight the issues I do and urge liberals to take them even more seriously than they perhaps have done in the past; to engage in that continuing self-criticism and growth that are essential to religious as well as to human maturity.

There are two categories in my agenda, one epistemological and one ontological. The first I shall call "relativity and reason" and the second "ecology and creatureliness." The latter opens out onto three important topics which I shall be able only to touch on: the problem of God, human bondage and freedom, and absurdity and death.

2. Relativity and Reason

"Post-modern" or broadly relativistic perspectives on epistemology, and through it on ontology, have been around throughout the twentieth century; but during the past twenty years or so they have come to assert themselves philosophically with new freshness and vigor. Where it has been fully alert to and engaged with the contemporary debate, liberal religious thought in America has had to begin coming to terms with post-modernism. There is no reason to think that this obligation will be any less urgent in the years ahead.

For the title of this section I have used the term "relativity" rather than "relativism," and I have spoken of "broadly relativistic" approaches to problems of knowledge and being. I do so because--if I may be permitted the linguistic indulgence--"relativism" is a somewhat "relative" term. A fully consistent philosophical and conceptual relativism must affirm the social or individual subjectivity and deny the objectivity and universality of all claims to knowledge and value--including, of course, its own definitive claims about relativism. In this full-blown sense, of course, there have been virtually no consistent relativists. The great "relativistic" social scientists of the first part of the twentieth century such as Ernst Troeltsch and Ruth Benedict focused on the cultural conditionedness of axiological beliefs and practices and exempted their own scientific assumptions, methods, and conclusions; and that has been a familiar pattern. In philosophy, Bertrand Russell and A. J. Ayer were as ardent in their acceptance of the normativity of scientific knowledge as they were in their denial of any universality (and indeed of any cognitive significance) to moral judgments, with their "emotivist" theories of ethics.

But we miss the enduring point of the older relativisms if we dwell on the fact that they were not consistent. Their lasting legacy is to have exposed decisively the indefinitely large extent to which our actual human choices in the realms of meanings, values, and behavior are shaped by cultural context and, within that context, by individual differences of temperament and character. *This* broadly relativistic challenge is very much alive and well, and to my mind has yet to be comprehensively and foundationally dealt with. The challenge to universality and objectivity in those axiological dimensions where most of us live most of the time directly affects the disciplines of philosophy and theology as well as of ethics. To this day it is striking how few theological writings address themselves to the far-reaching theological implications of the obvious fact that the reason Christianity rather than Buddhism is what Will James called a "living option" for me is that I am American rather than Burmese. H. Richard Niebuhr remains one of the very small number of theologians who have tackled these issues head-on, and the knowledgeable and creative way in which he did is a major reason why he is perhaps the most important American theologian of the twentieth century.[1]

More radical forms of relativism have become prominent during the past twenty-five years. The three most significant are the contextual analysis of language pioneered by Ludwig Wittgenstein; the revival of the pragmatist epistemologies of William James, C. S. Peirce, and John Dewey; and the sociology of knowledge with its roots in the work of Karl Marx, Max Scheler, Karl Mannheim, and George Herbert Mead. Representative of Wittgensteinian analysis have been such contemporary writers as Thomas Kuhn in the philosophy of the natural sciences, Peter Winch in the philosophy of the social sciences, and D. Z.

---

[1]See, e.g., *The Meaning of Revelation* (New York: Macmillan, 1941).

Phillips in the philosophy of religion and ethics.[2] Of neo-pragmatism it suffices to mention Richard Rorty's widely discussed and controversial rethinking of the philosophical tradition, *Philosophy and the Mirror of Nature*.[3] In North America perhaps the best-known exponent of the sociology of knowledge is Peter Berger, who co-authored (with Thomas Luckmann) *The Social Construction of Reality*.[4] I might have added to these deconstruction, which insofar as I can comprehend it appears to be a thoroughly relativistic approach to the hermeneutical task.

These recently prominent forms of relativism or "perspectivism" have forcefully reminded us of what seem to be inescapable features of human knowing. They reaffirm the insight, stemming from Kant, that all experience is interpreted experience, that human knowing is an intending, constructing, willing, value-laden activity. They illuminate the fact that all this constructive activity is irreducibly intersubjective, imbedded in social and linguistic contexts, communities, or "forms of life." As a mode of knowledge, scientific inquiry is not exempt from this analysis. The "new" relativists point to those dramatic "paradigm shifts" (Kuhn) that constitute scientific advance, when what has perhaps for centuries been regarded as "assured knowledge" of features of the natural order is exploded or at least relativized in the light of a new paradigm--but of course the shift does not take place until the new paradigm is generally accepted by the scientific community.

To take seriously the critical insights of the various forms of relativism is in no sense an argument for subjectivism, but rather for modesty and openness in the search for truth. It remains the case that there are correct and incorrect forms of reasoning; and there is a considerable body of empirical knowledge the validity of which it would be an unwarranted skepticism to deny. Rational knowledge of the world is indeed corrigible, but not infinitely so; the structures of the world are themselves a stable and limiting factor.

But liberal religion has characteristically had a strong investment in reason and science. Its traditional self-confidence about their ability to yield universal metaphysical and axiological truths still needs the chastening of the older relativists.

---

[2]See, e.g., Kuhn, *The Structure of Scientific Revolutions*, 2nd ed. (Chicago: University of Chicago Press, 1970); Winch, *The Ideal of a Social Science and its Relation to Philosophy* (London: Routledge & Kegan Paul, 1958); and Phillips, *Faith and Philosophical Enquiry* (London: Routledge & Kegan Paul, 1970).

[3](Princeton: Princeton University Press, 1979).

[4](New York: Anchor Books, 1967).

And liberalism's tendencies to absolutize scientific methods and conclusions need to be humbly attentive to the warnings and correctives of the new relativists. I hope that my own ontological reflections in the following section are on the one hand grounded in universal perceptions and evidence, and on the other hand sufficiently open and formalized to allow for a rich variety of concrete articulation.

3. Ecology and Creatureliness

I have become increasingly persuaded that the single most important foundational element in a theology and an ethics for the present and future is the fact of our utter creatureliness as human beings. With or without God, human beings are intrinsically and inescapably creatures among myriad creatures within a cosmic context that is for all practical purposes infinite. We are bound together with all beings in a relationship of total interdependence, from the microscopic to the macroscopic level. We are finite, and our most distinctively human ways of being never escape that finitude. Death is the inevitable wall and mystery surrounding our interdependence and finitude, the ultimate fact of our creatureliness within the horizons of space and time. At the same time, we humans are the creature who characterisically seeks to deny its creatureliness in often tragic and increasingly dangerous ways.

To be a creature is to be created, brought into being and sustained by other powers and processes, not self-caused and self-perpetuating. A creature is thus a contingent and contextual reality: its origin, continued existence, and activity always dependent upon and interdependent with a complex creaturely system that both pre-exists and survives it. Closely bound up with--indeed, contained within-- this contingency are limitation and transiency. To be a creature--even a "rational animal"--is to be limited in being, finite, with all that that entails regarding the scope of its knowledge and its activity. To be a contingent being is furthermore to be temporal: to have come into being and, so far at least as our observation can tell, to pass out of being. Within the parameters of "was not" and "will not be," the transiency of creatures is also a ceaseless process of change: the being of creatures is inexorably becoming.

I am concerned here with the crucial importance of recognizing, and of religiously and theologically building upon, *human* creatureliness, which however unique is a form of animal life within the planetary and cosmic ecology. As I intimated at the outset of this section, it is not necessary to believe in a Creator in order to acknowledge our ineradicable creatureliness. Our totally dependent and interdependent human status as creatures bound together with other creatures "great and small" is an inherent fact of our existence, with or without a "Lord God" who "made them all" as the old hymn goes on to say. It is furthermore a fact the denial and evasion of which has had and continues to have disastrous consequences for individuals and societies. The word "creature" and its derivatives, and their universal application to all finite beings, need to enter our secular along with our religious vocabulary. The concept of creatureliness is integral to a humane wisdom.

There are two types of the experience of creatureliness: the supernaturalistic and the naturalistic. To experience creatureliness in the context of divine creative powers or of a "higher" spiritual dimension of reality belongs to the supernaturalistic type. To experience our creatureliness entirely in the context of nature or the physical cosmos is the naturalist type. Clearly these two types reflect the interpretative element in the ways we experience our creatureliness. In the present discussion I do not want to venture into that complex issue. I wish only to point out that the two types of creature-experience have many elements in common, and the description of the concept of creatureliness with which I began applies to both. Both types are also capable of contributing to a contemporary wisdom.

In his book *A Common Faith*, speaking from a naturalistic but religious perspective which he called a "natural piety," John Dewey articulated some of the common elements in the supernatural and natural experiences of creatureliness so admirably that I can do no better than to quote his remarks at length:

> . . . There is no doubt . . . of our dependence upon forces beyond our control. Primitive man was so impotent in the face of these forces that, especially in an unfavorable natural environment, fear became a dominant attitude, and, as the old saying goes, fear created the gods.
>
> With increase of mechanisms of control [in the modern West], the element of fear has, relatively speaking, subsided. . . . But every crisis, whether of the individual or of the community, reminds man of the precarious and partial nature of the control he exercises. When man, individually and collectively, has done his uttermost, conditions that at different times and places have given rise to the ideas of Fate and Fortune, of Chance and Providence,

remain. It is the part of manliness to insist upon the capacity of mankind to strive to direct natural and social forces to humane ends. But unqualified absolutistic statements about the omnipotence of such endeavors reflect egoism rather than intelligent courage.

The fact that human destiny is so interwoven with forces beyond human control renders it unnecessary to suppose that dependence and the humility that accompanies it have to find the particular channel that is prescribed by traditional doctrines. . . . The essentially unreligious attitude is that which attributes human achievement and purpose to man in isolation from the world of physical nature and his fellows. Our successes are dependent upon the cooperation of nature. The sense of the dignity of human nature is as religious as is the sense of awe and reverence when it rests upon a sense of human nature as a cooperating part of a larger whole.[5]

These words are perhaps even more poignantly and acutely fresh today than they were in 1934, as the truth slowly but graphically dawns on us that the price of our long and ruthless denial of our creaturely interdependence through the *hubris* of energy squandering, pollution, overpopulation, great-power struggles, and the nuclear arms race is at last coming due.

Dewey's observations are underscored and brought into sharp focus for liberal religion by Larry Axel of Purdue University in his article "Religious Possibilities Since 1945: An Empirical Approach." There he argues that in the light of appalling events and possibilities of our time, epitomized and symbolized by the Holocaust and Hiroshima, not only traditional theism but also traditional humanism is dead. All varieties of liberal religious thought have defined themselves as humanistic, and non-theistic versions of religious liberalism have tended to espouse humanism as an alternative to theism. Axel characterizes this latter orientation as follows:

Some forms of humanism highlight the human structure as the most advanced of the many structures to emerge on this planet. The place reserved for God in many earlier religions is given now to humankind. Humanity's achievements are celebrated, its creativity and ability are lauded, its improvement and progress from earlier primitive organizations are documented, and its development toward greater future goods is confidently anticipated.

---

[5](New Haven: Yale University Press, 1934), 24-25.

One might add that even theistic varieties of liberal religious thought have shared to a large degree in this basically optimistic anthropocentricity.

But on the basis of empirical data which should be obvious to anyone who has eyes to see, Axel poses to religious liberals the sobering proposition that those sorts of humanism are challenged even more radically than are traditional theisms:

> It has long been recognized that the events of these years [1933-45] pose a real dilemma for the theist. But do they not pose a bigger problem for the humanist? Must not anyone who has encountered the intentional suffering and destruction of Auschwitz, Dachau, Hiroshima, and Nagasaki (and hundreds of similar episodes in human history) conclude that it would be blasphemous to worship humanity? A true empiricist, one who is open to the facts which everyone can discern, cannot easily engage in an idealizing of the human structure, and, of course, can hardly engage in making a deity of that structure. To the empiricist the achievements of humanity can scarcely serve as adequate material for a religion; the activities of contemporary humankind can hardly be praised in contrast to those of primitive peoples. The inquirer open to the empirical evidence must call for an end to human arrogance. It is certainly non-empirical and ignorant--if not blasphemous--to laud humanity as the crowning glory of the universe.

If the only two religious possibilities after 1945 are the traditional (and still generally pervasive) forms of theism and humanism, Axel concludes, then "there are no legitimate religious possibilities after 1945." But Axel goes on in a tantalizingly brief final paragraph to call religious liberals to move beyond such a dualism into a third alternative, which he calls a "religious creaturalism":

> . . . we must move beyond a dualism which sets the human apart from other creatures and structures, just as God was set radically apart in the older theisms. . . . Can we free ourselves from perspectives of domination as we try to do theology, as we live and think and have our being in a collaborative, relational way with nature, with one another, and with other creatures? Along this path we are not particularly confident of our way; we are not clear as to what kind of "religious" position we might be led. But *we must regain a sense of ourselves as one creatural structure among many of the earth, as participating ambiguously in the pathos, majesty and creaturehood of the universe as a whole.* To be sure, this is only a beginning. But a beginning which includes an end of arrogance and

creatural separation is no small step, indeed.[6]

Axel would be the first to acknowledge that in calling for a "religious creaturalism" he is by no means saying something new. Over the past decade environmental concern has caused a widespread theological revaluation and reaffirmation of the ecological dimensions of religion. What is particularly useful about Axel's presentation is the way he clearly poses the issue for religious liberals in terms of the still-common dualism between theism and humanism, and casts the alternative in terms of a recovery of a human sense of creatureliness. In this he stands in a significant tradition of theological interpretation which looks to such pioneering thinkers as Alfred North Whitehead and Henry Nelson Wieman.

I believe that the focus on and exploration of creatureliness can furnish the widest and soundest basis upon which to develop new forms of "natural theology" in American liberal religious thought. The total interdependence of both human and non-human realities is a planetary and cosmic fact for which there is overwhelming empirical verification from the natural and social sciences and ordinary observation. It is also the inescapable context of all human search for and reflection upon ultimate reality, of all human desires and values. Just as the challenge of epistemological relativism can both enlarge liberalism's horizons and deepen its intellectual humility, so also can close ontological attention to human creatureliness in its many dimensions and varied implications provide liberalism with a holistic and realistic philosophical-theological framework and a corrective for whatever tendencies liberalism has had in the direction of a one-sided and truncated "humanism." In the remainder of this essay I want to touch very briefly on three examples of central issues for the future of American liberal theology which I believe are imposed upon us by the overarching fact of creatureliness: the problem of God, human bondage and freedom, and absurdity and death.

1. "Creature-feeling" (Rudolf Otto) and the more general human sense of contingency have been indissolubly linked to the idea of God in traditional religious faith and thought. By contrast, modern liberal religious thought has had a divided mind on the connection. On one side has been liberalism in the Kantian tradition, which has shared Kant's metaphysical skepticism and dealt with the problem of

---

[6]In *Kairos: An Independent Quarterly of Liberal Religion*, 29:5, 1983. Italics added.

God only or very largely in terms of the "practical reason" broadly and variously conceived. This is the tradition of thinkers otherwise as varied as Albrecht Ritschl, Wilhelm Herrmann, Rudolf Bultmann, Shailer Mathews, and E. S. Ames. On the other side have been the naturalist and "process" traditions which have continued in various ways to deal with the problem of God squarely in relation to the natural order. One thinks in this connection of Whitehead, Wieman, Bernard Meland, Charles Hartshorne, John Cobb, and Marjorie Suchocki. Clearly the dichotomy described above is by no means absolute; and God as living redeemer and focus of values is surely central and essential to theistic forms of faith. But I want to suggest that the all-embracing reality of creaturely interdependence makes the omission or neglect of the relationship of God to nature simply untenable for future theological reflection. To envision God entirely as human liberator, as source or ideal focus of human values, or as protagonist in certain mythopoetically articulated "forms of life" is yet another version of an unacceptably one-dimensional and unrealistic "humanism." Creatureliness as a foundation for theological reflection will require liberal religious thought to deal fully with human existence in inextricable relationship to its planetary and cosmic ecology, and thus with God as inescapably bound up with nature as well as with us.

The question *how* God is to be understood relative to the natural order is of course one on which there is and will continue to be fruitful ongoing debate within American liberal religious thought. Broadly speaking, that debate is between conceptualizing God as creative processes within nature (Wieman) and as creative transcendent-immanent context of nature (process theology). I cannot go into the complexities of the debate here. I would only observe that it seems to me that on the basis of the creaturely reality of total planetary and cosmic interdependence, God as envisioned by Wieman, despite his careful qualifications, is delimited too anthropocentrically and lacks the ultimacy which has until comparatively recently been regarded as intrinsic to the logic of "God."

2. If there is one thread running with complete consistency through the history of American liberal religion, it is the theme of human freedom. Unfortunately, religious liberals' use of that tortured and equivocated term has been as long on rhetoric and short on analysis as most other people's. An important twofold challenge of the future for liberal religious thought in America is (a) to come more seriously to grips than we have hitherto with the large measure of

unfreedom or bondage in human behavior and what we are to make of it theologically; and (b) to develop clearer and more careful understandings of human freedom and ethics guided by empirical realities.

Our creaturely dependence and interdependence are not only external but internal, built into our very bone and psychic marrow. Both outer and inner nature are the fruitful condition of all the goods we know, but they are also the indifferent source of our oppression and suffering. External nature both nurtures and destroys. Internal (human) nature is to an indefinitely large degree the product of the complex interaction of genetic coding and social environment, expressing itself in creative but also in appallingly destructive ways. In both its personal and its social dimensions human life is at best a fruitful interdependence and at worst a vicious bondage.

What makes the present world situation and future prospects cause for uneasiness is not that we are any more victims of our internal compulsions and conflicts than people have ever been, but that we have so much greater power to destroy. These insights that are the enduring legacy of Freud and depth psychology are repeatedly confirmed by honest introspection and observation. American liberal religious thought, with its own legacy of optimism, must in a future that is at least as much a source of apprehension as of hope come more radically and seriously to grips than ever before with the depth of human bondage. We must attend more carefully and empirically to the problems of freedom and responsibility, and develop modes of ethical discourse and action appropriate to both the "weightedness" and the possibilities of the human condition. We have a specific theological responsibility to explore with clear-eyed honesty the disturbing connections between human bondage and the problem of God, whether God is viewed as context of nature or as processes within nature.

3. It was Albert Camus who unforgettably called attention to another central feature of our uniquely human creatureliness, with his formulation of the notion of "absurdity." In *The Myth of Sisyphus*[7] he begins with the two poles, human beings and the world. On one side there is the world--by which Camus seems to mean our nonhuman environment, both this planet as we locally experience it and

---

[7]*The Myth of Sisyphus and Other Essays*, trans. Justin O'Brien (New York: Alfred A. Knopf, 1955).

58

the universe of which it is a tiny part. The world, he says, is "irrational," in the sense that it does not yield rational answers to our most basic and urgent human questions about the world and ourselves: Why is there something rather than nothing? Is there a final, ultimate meaning to the world and our lives? and if so, what is it? To these questions the universe is silent, and Camus is concerned in *Sisyphus* to show that all human attempts to answer them are not rationally demonstrable explanations but acts of faith. In an interesting way his insights here make connection with the problem of relativism which I discussed earlier.

On the other side of the dipolarity we have human beings--the strange animal cast up by the evolutionary process. "Strange" because we are apparently the only creature on earth who demands more of life than it seems to be able to get. With our remarkable cognitive capacities, particularly our ability to symbolize, and our self-awareness, we try in myriad ways to wrest ultimate meaning, unity, clarity, and fulfillment from the world. In art, myth, religion, ideology, and philosophy, we seek final explanations or coherence, which will unify and make sense out of both our human life and the context in which it is set. This deep-seated hunger or longing--this "nostalgia," as Camus describes it--for ultimate significance and harmony, lies at the very heart of the uniquely human experience.

Neither the world nor *homo sapiens* the strange animal is in itself absurd. The absurd, says Camus, is precisely the *relationship* between humans with their demand for ultimate meaning and the irrational world: the "confrontation between the human need and the unreasonable silence of the world."[8] It is a relationship that is also a divorce, an incommensurability. Insofar as human beings experience themselves as other than their natural environment and as wanting more than it can yield, they experience to that degree a certain amount of alienation or exile from the world. This then is the absurdity of the human condition: nature has produced a being with needs that nature cannot fulfill. The juxtaposition of the human need for ultimate meaning with the ultimate lack of meaning yielded by the universe is the absurd situation. Death is the inexorable "absurd wall" of our condition, the universal necessity against which we ceaselessly employ many stratagems but finally in vain. Death is the ultimate fact and reminder of our creaturely absurdity.

It is easy to overdramatize the whole idea of absurdity. But there is a sense

---

[8]P. 21.

in which Camus rightly chose a word with its drama and shock value. Far too many forms of nineteenth- and twentieth-century humanism and naturalism--and indeed of liberal religion--have tended to gloss over the sober truth about what the human situation in the world really is when considered apart from a theologically or philosophically transcendent realm. With their various optimisms about the reorganization of human society and the possibilities of technology, they prefer not to remind us of a few bedrock facts yielded by their assumptions: that we are creatures blindly produced by the evolutionary process who demand ultimate meaning to our existence but tragically encounter only the unreasoning silence of nature; that we suffer the vicissitudes of heredity, environment, and one another without recourse or hope for their eventual rectification; that we die and that is the end of our brief appearance on a small planet in an incomprehensibly vast and impersonal universe.

Camus unforgettably dramatizes for those who have left behind the traditional consolations of religion in favor of fully this-worldly alternatives--whether religious or non-religious--what really lies at the bottom, underneath such varied window dressings as evolutionary naturalism, Marxism, or ethical humanism. It is the special courage of Camus to have stripped away all the masks, stared the absurd situation in the face, and with full consciousness of it as his ultimate frame of reference to have carved out in his life and writings an honest and creative affirmation of human meaning and values. The same urgent obligation rests upon liberal religious thought and any who wish to rely as fully and candidly as possible on reason and experience.

The singular role that death plays in dramatizing the absurd situation needs special attention from those liberal religious thinkers who have perhaps preserved intact an ultimate context of meaning and value, as in the God of process theologies, but who have given up any notion of life after death. *Hope* has become a central category in contemporary theology, prominently in the liberation theologies. The phenomenologies typically associated with such theologies affirm that hope is essential to human existence. But the future in which liberation theologies are interested is to a very large degree an intramundane and political future, not eternal life. Much liberal theology is characterized by outright skepticism about or rejection of the hope of human rectification and fulfillment beyond death, and likewise prefers to speak of this-worldly possibilities. Insofar as American liberal religious thought views the human situation entirely within the boundaries of birth and death, it will as it looks to its own future have to deal much more seriously than it has with the question: What does liberal religion have to say to people whose situation is hopeless? Does it have anything to all to say? Is it so fixated on hope and future that it cannot affirm the meaningfulness of human life without hope? To put it concretely: Is liberal theology capable of affirming human significance in the face of terminal illness, age-old forms of unrelieved human misery, and nuclear or environmental catastrophe?

The late Walter Kaufmann of Princeton was one of our most refreshing gadflies when it came to challenging widely-held intellectual assumptions. In one of his profounder essays, "Existentialism and Death," he dealt refreshingly with the problem of hope in the face of death:

> The Greeks . . . considered hope the final evil in Pandora's box. They also gave us an image of perfect nobility: a human being lovingly doing her duty to another human being despite all threats, and going to her death with pride and courage, not deterred by any hope--Antigone.

> It may seem that a man without hope is inhuman. How can one appeal to him if he does not share our hopes? He has pulled up his stakes in the future--and the future is the common ground of humanity. Such rhetoric may sound persuasive, but Antigone gives it the lie. Nobility holds to a purpose when hope is gone. Purpose and hope are as little identical as humility and meekness, or honesty and sincerity. Hope seeks redemption in time to come and depends on the future. A purposive act may be its own reward and redeem the agent, regardless of what the future may bring. Antigone is not at the mercy of any future. Humanity, love, and courage survive hope.[9]

There is both an ethics and a theology implied in these words, and religious liberals would do well to ponder them. They furnish a fitting conclusion to my sobering remarks on the reality of creatureliness as the all-embracing agenda as American liberal religious thought moves into an uncertain future. That agenda will demand an intellectual and moral humility in the face of the pluralism and tentativeness of

---

[9]In *Existentialism, Religion, and Death: Thirteen Essays* (New York: New American Library, 1976), 213, 215.

our philosophical and theological perspectives; an unflinching honesty in coming to grips with our human and cosmic condition that moves beyond "humanism"; and a creative imagination that can both persuade and inspire with a worthy vision of life. To embody those qualities will have been no mean achievement.

Chapter 5

American Feminist Theology and the American Pragmatist Tradition

Among the many virtues of feminist theologies is a preoccupation with and forthrightness about methodology. In my reading of feminist theologians I have been struck by the parallels I think I have seen between their methods and what William James called the "pragmatic method" in philosophy. In fact, I am prepared to argue that examining the feminist theological enterprise in terms of the pragmatic method illuminates the very heart of its theo-logic and confirms why truly woman-affirming forms of theological reflection should take some such form.

I speak rather grandly in my title about "the American Pragmatist Tradition," but I will focus only on William James and more specifically still on his 1906-07 lectures entitled *Pragmatism.* Likewise I refer in my title to "American Feminist Theology," but I will restrict myself to certain themes in representative writings of a few well-known feminist theologians. What I am doing here is only a very preliminary attempt to follow up on some suggestions Sarah Trulove and I made in the concluding part of our 1986 essay "The Feminist Re-formation of American Religious Thought." We tried briefly to suggest some connections between American feminist theology and that stream in the history of American religious though exemplified by thinkers such as Emerson and James which strongly emphasized the validation of religious ideas in concrete experience.[1]

One further qualification: I am highlighting certain feminist theological methods as exemplifying the spirit of what James called the pragmatic method. I am not making a case for historical influence but only for certain significant parallels. The occasional mention of a name or the influence of an idea such as we find for example in the writings of Mary Daly, who is always careful to mention her sources, is not in itself sufficient to make any sort of case for an intellectual-historical "lineage."

Let me try to summarize James's characterization of pragmatism in his lectures on the subject, ending up with the implications he saw for theology:

1. Pragmatism is a method of approaching problems, not a particular set of results. "The pragmatic method," James writes, "is to try to interpret each notion by tracing its respective practical consequences. What difference would it practically make to any one if this notion rather than that notion were true? If no practical difference whatever can be traced, then the alternatives mean practically the same thing, and all dispute is idle. Whenever a dispute is serious, we ought to be able to show some practical difference that must follow from one side or the other's being right."[2]

2. The pragmatic method manifests the "empiricist attitude" rather than the mind-set of rationalism, although not in the often narrow sense of nineteenth-century scientific empiricism or twentieth-century positivism. The pragmatist, James says, "turns away from abstraction and insufficiency, from verbal solutions, from bad *a priori* reasons, from fixed principles, closed systems, and pretended absolutes and origins. He turns towards concreteness and adequacy, towards facts, towards action and towards power. . . .It means the open air and possibilities of nature, as against dogma, artificiality, and the pretense of finality in truth." (25) Although James maintains in the Preface to *Pragmatism* that "there is no logical connexion" between pragmatism and what he calls "radical empiricism" (4), there is at least a close material connection, as we can see from his description of the pragmatic method as exhibiting a richly rather than a narrowly empiricist mentality.

---

[1] In Peter Freese, ed., *Religion and Philosophy in the United States of America*, vol. 2 (Essen: Verlag die blaue Eule, 1987), 748-753.

[2] *Pragmatism and Other Essays* (New York: Washington Square Press, 1963), 23. All further page references will appear in parentheses in the text.

3. The pragmatic orientation to experiential consequences treats theories as instruments to enable us to organize and make our way intelligently around in our experience, not as ends in themselves. This embodies a certain theory of truth, the "instrumentalist" view for which the pragmatists are of course well known. As James characterizes it, "ideas (which themselves are but parts of our experience) become true just in so far as they help us to get into satisfactory relations with other parts of our experience, to summarize them and get about among them by conceptual short-cuts instead of following the interminable succession of particular phenomena." (28)

4. The implications of pragmatism for religion and theology are positive and creative. James, who was of course continually preoccupied with these implications, states them succinctly in *Pragmatism*: "Now pragmatism, devoted though she be to facts, has no such materialistic bias as ordinary empiricism labors under. . . .Interested in conclusions but those which our minds and our experiences work out together, she has no *a priori* prejudices against theology. If theological ideas prove to have a value for concrete life, they will be true, for pragmatism, in the sense of being good for so much. For how much more they are true, will depend entirely on their relations to the other truths that also have to be acknowledged." (35)

These four characteristics of pragmatism constitute, I believe, an illuminating angle of vision on American feminist theological methods. Let me suggest how the pragmatic method is exemplified in feminist theologies.

The testing of metaphysical and moral ideas on the basis of their practical consequences, when applied to theological method, is essential to the work of feminist theologians. They critically examine and often reject or revise inherited theological images and concepts on the basis of the marginalizing and dehumanizing effect they have had and continue to have on women. At the same time feminist theologians constructively "re-vision" the entire theological agenda in the light of women's experience and empowerment.

We can see this "consequentialism" in the development of feminist theological norms. In *Beyond God the Father*, Mary Daly explicitly invoked James's pragmatism in enunciating a normative principle for evaluating theological language: ". . . I am employing a pragmatic yardstick or verification process to God-language in a manner not totally dissimilar to that of William James. In my thinking, the specific criterion which implies a mandate to reject certain forms of God-talk is expressed in the question: Does this language hinder human becoming by reinforcing sex-role socialization? Expressed positively. . . : Does it *encourage* human becoming toward psychological and social fulfillment, toward an androgynous mode of living, toward transcendence?"[3] Daly is well known for her insistence that feminist thought and action must be ontologically grounded, and in developing an ontology in *Beyond God the Father* and her later books she has been guided by what I have called the pragmatist principle just cited. She found in Paul Tillich's characterization of God as "the ground and power of being" the beginnings of a religious ontology that could ground the empowerment of women through existential courage by which the threat of "nonbeing" is overcome and human potentialities actualized. Women's true selves are rooted in the dynamic power of Be-ing, an ultimate grounding which endures the destructive foreground of patriarchy.

Rosemary Ruether, in *Sexism and God-Talk*, expresses what she calls the "critical principle" of feminist theology in similarly pragmatic terms: "The critical principle of feminist theology is the promotion of the full humanity of women. . . .whatever diminishes or denies the full humanity of women must be presumed not to reflect the divine or an authentic relation to the divine, or to reflect the authentic nature of things, or to be the message or work of an authentic redeemer or a community of redemption."[4] Ruether here makes it quite explicit that what James called "practical consequences" are the test of theological truth or falsity, when she speaks of woman-diminishing ideas as not reflecting "the authentic nature of things."

The work of Elisabeth Schüssler Fiorenza has been directed specifically to developing a feminist biblical hermeneutic for "women-church." In her book *Bread Not Stone* she locates the criteria for biblical interpretation in "women-church" itself: "Its vision of liberation and salvation is informed by the biblical texts under the authority of feminist experience insofar as it maintains that revelation is ongoing

---

[3]*Beyond God the Father: Toward a Philosophy of Women's Liberation* (Boston: Beacon Press, 1973), 21.

[4]*Sexism and God-Talk: Toward a Feminist Theology* (Boston: Beacon Press, 1983), 18-19.

and takes place 'for the sake of our salvation.'"[5] Throughout *Bread Not Stone* Schüssler Fiorenza applies this contemporary norm to a variety of hermeneutical and theological issues.

The "empiricist attitude" that James described as a feature of the pragmatic method seems to me to be integral to the approaches of American feminist theologies. In saying this I do not want to draw specific connections between what I would call their broadly empiricist orientation and the details of James's doctrine of "radical empiricism" as set forth in his *Essays on Radical Empiricism*.[6] What we find in feminist theological method is however a radical commitment, in James's words, to "concreteness. . . , facts, . . .action and. . .power."[7] Feminist theologians characteristically set over against what they see as the other-worldliness and abstraction of the patriarchal tradition, a serious and loving attention to the world of concrete experience--to our bodily existence as members of society and participants in the natural world. They seek to be attentive to human experience in fresh and holistic ways, to bring to it new and neglected interpretations, and always to remain close to its concreteness in their imaging and conceptualizing of the divine. Very importantly, for American feminist theologians theological reflection on experience is one side of a *praxis* the other side of which is liberating action-- empowerment--in dialectical relationship with the reflection.

Among many examples that might be mentioned here, I will refer only to Judith Plaskow's early book *Sex, Sin and Grace: Women's Experience and the Theologies of Reinhold Niebuhr and Paul Tillich*. It is a thorough analysis and critique of two influential twentieth-century theological anthropologies on the basis of a careful attempt to characterize women's experience in the light of psychosocial observation and theory and literary exploration. In her conclusion Plaskow summarizes the importance of such an approach to enriching our understanding of the human: "If what is common in human experience can be discerned only through the particularities of experience, it becomes the obligation of groups from which little has been heard to articulate their own experience and contribute their perceptions to a multi-faceted theological exploration of experience. . . .the

---

[5]*Bread Not Stone: The Challenge of Feminist Biblical Interpretation* (Boston: Beacon Press, 1984), 14.

[6](New York: E. P. Dutton, Inc., 1971).

[7]*Pragmatism and Other Essays*, 25.

submerged perspective of women's experience, once brought to expression, precisely in its particularity has the power to direct our attention to previously unexplored aspects of human experience."[8] I think James would have found this sort of concrete, pluralistic approach to building up our knowledge of the universally human quite congenial.

At the level of epistemology we find in American feminist theologies assumptions that echo emphases of the earlier American pragmatists, although they are articulated in the terms of the more recent American discussion centering in the ideas of philosophers such as Thomas Kuhn, Richard Rorty, and Richard Bernstein. Feminist theologians are particularly drawn to the critique of foundationalism, the "relativizing" of theory by experience, the formulation of the notion of paradigms and paradigm shifts in the development of thought, and the essential role that what Bernstein calls "dialogical community" plays in adjudicating what is true and false.

In *Bread Not Stone* Schüssler Fiorenza provides an explicit epistemological rationale for the development of a feminist biblical hermeneutics. Building on Richard Bernstein's *Beyond Objectivism and Relativism*--which incorporates the work of Rorty, Kuhn, Gadamer, and Habermas--she describes her own project as follows: "I have argued. . .that rather than seek a 'revealed' Archimedean point in the shifting sand of biblical-historical relativity--be it a liberating tradition, text, or principle in the Bible--a feminist critical hermeneutics has to explore and assess whether and how Scripture can become an enabling, motivating resource and empowering authority in women's struggle for justice, liberation, and solidarity."[9] She goes on to give concrete application to Bernstein's idea of "dialogical communities" as the practical-moral context that grounds rational discussion "beyond objectivism and relativism." Schüssler Fiorenza writes that "whereas such dialogical communities remain for Bernstein a *telos* that he cannot name concretely and identify historically, I have put forward women-church as the dialogical community that is incipiently given but still needs to be realized in feminist conversion and historical struggle for liberation from patriarchal oppression."[10]

Elsewhere Schüssler Fiorenza applies Thomas Kuhn's theory of paradigms

---

[8](Lanham, MD: University Press of America, 1980), 174-175.
[9]*Bread Not Stone*, xxiii.
[10]P. xxiv.

to theological construction and development: "The usefulness of this theory for theology and the community of faith is obvious. The theory shows the historically conditioned nature of all scientific investigation. It also maintains that a language of neutral observation is not possible, that all scientific investigation demands commitment and a community of persons dedicated to a particular perspective. Moreover, it helps us understand that theological approaches, like all other scientific theories, are not falsified but are often replaced, not because we find new 'data,' but because we find a new way of looking at old data."[11] This approach to an epistemological grounding for theology has been more fully elaborated by Sallie McFague in such books as *Metaphorical Theology*.

While not always formulated so directly, ideas such as these make up the epistemological context of American feminist theologies. Their content and their connection with the contemporary philosophical discussion link them to an epistemological tradition pioneered by James, Peirce, and Dewey.

In this essay I have tried to suggest in a brief and sketchy manner, some of the ways in which it appears that American feminist theologies exhibit what James called the pragmatic method: in their testing the truth of theological images and ideas by criteria taken from women's experience of empowerment, in their broadly empiricist commitment to the fullness of concrete experience and to theological interpretations that remain close to it, and in their epistemological tendencies in the direction of instrumentalism and contextualism.

To conclude: My reflections on the pragmatic method in American feminist theologies have prompted the wider realization that *most* of what might broadly be called American liberal theologies share methodologically in the American pragmatist legacy. It is just that the theological feminists have the merit of spelling it out with special clarity and force. As I have argued elsewhere, for most liberal theologies the real norm for testing and reconstructing images and ideas of God is their humanizing or dehumanizing consequences in human experience.[12] The widespread liberal rejection of exclusively patriarchal and generally authoritarian divine images and of concepts of divine omnipotence and omniscience manifest this more modest, experience-bound approach to theological reflection. Will James, of

---

11P. 24.
12See Chapter 3.

course, would have heartily approved of such modifications of Christian theism. As to epistemology, I do not think it is exaggerating to say that most contemporary liberal theologies have a vested interest in post-modernist versions of perspectivism and instrumentalism, just as their neo-orthodox forebears rejoiced in the anti-foundationalism of the existentialist philosophers.

When we survey the contemporary American theological scene, in fact, a good case could be made for characterizing it as at least the temporary triumph of a kind of neo-pragmatism. I have tried in the barest sort of way to argue that American feminist theology seems to be a reasonably clear example of this. I think there have been important gains in adopting a pragmatic method in theological reflection. I think there are also problems with the usual ways in which such a method is applied which I have not attempted to pursue within the limited scope of this essay.

Chapter 6

The Contextuality of Belief and Unbelief in "The Will to Believe."

In "The Will to Believe" and some of its sister essays in *The Will to Believe and Other Essays in Popular Philosophy*,[1] William James analyzed the issues between faith and skepticism in a manner that I believe remains generally persuasive today. The persuasiveness of his analysis lies in his perceptive illumination of the inescapable role of human desires and feelings and also of cultural context in our apprehension of the world generally, and their decisive role in moral, metaphysical, and religious questions. William Barrett speaks of James's "lifelong sensitivity to the hidden and subliminal sources of the human mind," of his "grasp of feeling as the central fact for any human life."[2] The classic summary-word is "sentiment," and one of the essays in *The Will to Believe and Other Essays* bears the eminently Jamesian title "The Sentiment of Rationality." In it he showed the feeling component in the experience of anything as "rational," and the elements of desire and faith at the very foundation of the scientific enterprise.[3] In those great issues of human existence which cannot be sufficiently adjudicated by scientific evidence-- morals, metaphysics, and religion--James argues that sentiment plays and should

---

[1](Cambridge, MA: Harvard University Press, 1979). Page references will appear in the text.

[2]*The Illusion of Technique* (Garden City, NY: Anchor Books, 1979), 278, 279.

[3]James, 57-89.

play an important role.

To anticipate our examination of "The Will to Believe," this attention to desire and feeling emphatically did not imply for James a subjectivism or radical skepticism about empirical knowledge generally. Paul van Buren puts it nicely: "In no way did James mean to denigrate facts or theories. . . . In no sense did he think it made no difference how we carved up our experienced world. But he did insist that however we went about this, the human element was always part of it and that our metaphysics ought to be honest about this."[4]

Like most of James's writings, "The Will to Believe" was originally a lecture; in this case, an address to the Philosophical Clubs of Yale and Brown Universities. It was published in the *New World* in June, 1896, and became in 1897 the title essay of a book of ten essays that were all originally lectures given largely to student groups over a period of almost twenty years.

Two matters need to be dealt with at the outset. One is the title of the essay, and the other is the intellectual context and issues to which James was addressing himself in *The Will to Believe and Other Essays* and in an important sense throughout his career. James lamented his choice of the title "The Will to Believe" many times in the years that followed its appearance. The theme of the essay is really the intellectual *right* to believe religiously. As he stated in its opening paragraphs, it was "an essay in justification of faith, a defense of our right to adopt a believing attitude in religious matters, in spite of the fact that our merely logical intellect may not have been coerced." (13) The use of the term "will" came from James's emphasis on the right of our "willing nature" (18) or inclinations to guide us in moral, metaphysical, and religious matters. He interpreted the term broadly to include a range of psychological states and also the influence of social context: "When I say 'willing nature' I do not mean only such deliberate volitions as may have set up habits of belief that we cannot now escape from--I mean all such factors of belief as fear and hope, prejudice and passion, imitation and partisanship, the circumpressure of our cast and set." (18) But making "will" the terminological centerpiece of the essay laid James open to misunderstanding and caricature, suggesting a "voluntarism" he did not really espouse.

---

[4]*Theological Explorations* (New York: The Macmillan Company, 1968), 150-151.

The fact that the essay is really a philosophical defense of our intellectual *right* to believe religiously is closely related to the intellectual context in which it was written. William James of course wrote during a period of great achievement and enormous self-confidence in the sciences. A common and often-repeated educated belief of the late nineteenth and early twentieth centuries was that science had provided us with a large body of assured knowledge of the world and ourselves, and in principle was sufficient to explain all spheres of human existence including ethics and religion. Scientific methods and conclusions were the only rational and reliable guide to truth. As Sigmund Freud, who remained committed to scientific rationalism even as he moved richly beyond it in his own work, summed it up: ". . . our science [unlike religion] is no illusion. But an illusion it would be to suppose that what science cannot give us we can get elsewhere."[5]

An important aspect of James's philosophical stature is that, thoroughly immersed in the science of his day as a physician and psychologist, he saw clearly and articulated powerfully the problematic character of these beliefs that dominated the intelligentsia of his time and were beginning to influence in popular form people's thinking generally. "The Will to Believe" and its companion essays were directed specifically at two leading British scientific agnostics, T. H. Huxley and W. K. Clifford--particularly the latter. In his much-discussed essay "The Ethics of Belief," Clifford had enunciated the principle that a person has a duty to be agnostic in religious matters because there is insufficient evidence for the truth of religious beliefs (and, he personally believed, considerable evidence against it). One is obligated at minimum to suspend judgment on religious beliefs.[6] James was considerably annoyed by what he regarded as the unwarranted assumptions and the arrogance of this position. James fully granted the *right* of a person to adopt a religiously agnostic outlook because of a scrupulous intellectual concern to proportion her or his ultimate beliefs strictly to the evidence, an inability to "let go" and follow her or his religious inclinations, or a lack of interest in religion as a live option. What he denied was that we have an intellectual *duty* to be religiously agnostic, and what he defended was our intellectual right (not of course our duty) to

[5]*The Future of an Illusion*, trans. and ed. James Strachey (New York: W. W. Norton & Co., 1962), 56.

[6]Reprinted in Gerald D. McCarthy, ed., *The Ethics of Belief Debate* (Atlanta: Scholars Press, 1986), 19-36.

adopt a believing attitude in religious matters.

It is important to see "The Will to Believe" and James's related essays in this historical and intellectual context. As he made quite clear, he was addressing university-educated persons in the late nineteenth century who were characteristically torn between a religious background and disposition on the one hand and the claims and criticisms of scientific knowledge on the other. In his inimitable way James was seeking to demythologize scientism and demonstrate on the basis of philosophical analysis that religious believing is a legitimate perspective on life and the world for an educated, reflective person to hold. Despite the passage of time and the many changes in both science and religion that have taken place since James's death, in my experience the conflict to which he addressed himself is played out again and again in each new generation of university students whose minds are challenged and broadened by exposure to a liberal education.

It is this context that John Hick entirely misses in his critique of "The Will to Believe" in *Faith and Knowledge* and other writings. He treats James as a representative of "voluntarist theories of faith," and then faults him because (among other things) faith as described in "The Will to Believe" is not the faith of the ordinary believer.[7] This is a complete misinterpretation. James was not setting forth a general theory of faith, as both his introductory remarks and the text of the essay make clear. The essay and its companion essays were explicitly directed at the particular, relatively small audience I have described and in response to the specific sorts of struggles they had and have with faith and doubt. What he does throughout the essay is perceptively to expose those general features of human life and knowledge which render faith a viable human option. But it is quite as obvious to James as it is to Hick that the faith of the large majority of religious believers throughout the world is a personal and cultural "given," a life-context something like the air they breathe, and not to be described as a "live option" since other options are not available or at least not considered.

William Barrett makes a mistake similar to Hick's, although somewhat less flat-footedly, when, criticizing James, he asks us to "imagine a man of faith, some peasant out of Tolstoy or Unamuno, who is suddenly accosted with the question, 'Do you believe in God?'. . . He might very well stare at you uncomprehendingly.

---

[7]*Faith and Knowledge* (Ithaca, NY: Cornell University Press, 1957), 48-57.

The question will seem just as odd as to ask him whether he believes in his own name. His relation to the faith in which he lives is not an epistemological relation to a proposition."[8] Barrett goes on to say that James's preoccupation with what he liked to call "the religious hypothesis" was accordingly "playing the wrong language game."[9] On the contrary: Again, in terms of the specific audience James was addressing--decidedly *not* Tolstoy's or Unamuno's peasants--an audience thoroughly imbued by the sciences with the vocabulary of "hypotheses," talking about the "religious hypothesis" was precisely the appropriate "language game" to play. Furthermore, despite his epistemological language, the whole burden of James's argument is to show that even for the liberally educated person, confronted with alternative perspectives on reality, the choice between faith and skepticism is a choice of the whole person in her or his concrete circumstances and not only intellectual assent to a proposition or a set of propositions.

But let us now turn directly to those aspects of the text of "The Will to Believe" that are pertinent to the subject of this essay. James begins by defining the terms of the discussion. *Hypothesis* will mean "anything that may be proposed to our belief." James then subdivides hypotheses into "live" and "dead" ones. "A live hypothesis is one which appeals as a real possibility to him to whom it is proposed." (14) Although James's definition of a hypothesis is a perfectly general one, he immediately distinguishes hypotheses on purely existential grounds as "live" and "dead" and determines liveness in hypotheses by a person's practical willingness to act on them. It is clear that this characterization applies with obvious force to moral and religious hypotheses: hypotheses which constitute what we might call our "primary beliefs" about reality and human conduct and which are of course precisely the most momentous and the most hotly disputed ones. Primary beliefs are surely, for those who are seriously related to them, the paradigm cases of live hypotheses, those that present themselves to us as real possibilities and inspire and guide our actions. It is worth highlighting at this point the intrinsic connection James sees between belief and practice.

Thus were are plunged at the very outset into the *concreteness, contingency,* and *contextuality* of human believing. For James's Protestant Christian Ivy League

---

[8]Barrett, 303.
[9]P. 304.

audience of a hundred years ago, belief in the Mahdi was decidedly not a live hypothesis. Despite the more recent popularization of knowledge of other religious traditions and the flowering of real and ersatz Asian religiosity in the West, for the vast majority even of well-educated Americans today it remains the case that Hindu deities and Buddhist dharma, together with all sorts of other possible objects of belief, simply do not constitute live hypotheses. For some, of course, the whole sphere of religious beliefs of whatever sort lies outside the pale of interest or concern. What our primary beliefs consist of and exclude is always conditioned, to an indefinitely large degree, by what our real personal and cultural alternatives are. I grew up a white, male, middle-class American Protestant Christian inclined to be intensely involved in religious issues, and not someone of a different sex, race, or temperament raised in a completely secularized working-class French household or in a devout Shi'ite Muslim peasant home in Iran. These social and personal contingencies are so obviously shapers and limiters of our primary beliefs that the indifference, resistance, and rationalization of even reflective believers and of theologians toward seriously pondering the implications of this fact might at first appear puzzling. Psychologically it is quite understandable, however, since these contextualities seem to constitute a relativistic abyss peering into which can produce extreme vertigo.

James, then, immediately draws our attention to the fact that our religious situation is inescapably pluralistic. Even that infinitesimally small number of human beings who are historians and philosophers of religion, with their much wider and more carefully reasoned grasp of the issues and the alternatives, remain *qua* believers strikingly predictable in the sorts of views that genuinely count as live hypotheses for them. Is it not revealingly significant that a John Hick, a Ninian Smart, a Mircea Eliade, an R. C. Zaehner are Christians, and that their highly informed and illuminating studies of global religion at times unmistakably exhibit what are usually called "Christian biases"?

James proceeds by introducing the term *option*, which he defines as "the decision between two hypotheses." (14) There are three sorts of options: (a) living or dead, (b) forced or avoidable, and (c) momentous or trivial. James then stipulates that what he calls a "genuine" option is one that is living, forced, and momentous. Here he moves into the crux of the issue for his educated American audience struggling between religious and skeptical hypotheses. As in the case of the definition of a hypothesis, James begins with a completely general characterization of an option but then immediately plunges us into the most crucial sorts of human options--the "genuine" ones. All the terms in the three kinds of options are existential or practical ones; they describe the relationship between the option and the person entertaining it. Only those options that are simultaneously living, forced, and momentous count as genuine, that is, as real and serious choices for the person making them.

A living or (as we would probably say) "live" option means that both hypotheses before us are live ones. "Christianity or Buddhism" is not a living option for a vast majority of Americans and Europeans. The former may represent a real possibility to many--a "live hypothesis"--but the latter only to a handful of people. James's "agnosticism or Christianity" hits perhaps closest to the mark in characterizing the concrete option for many searching, reflective persons. But from individual to individual even that is of course too broad. There are particular forms or expressions of Christianity, for example, that represent dead hypotheses for some persons: perhaps fundamentalist Protestantism, Mormonism, or the Jehovah's Witnesses. That does not mean that *no* forms of Christianity are live hypotheses for a person; and even when it does, it does not mean that some broad expression of faith in the supernatural may not be a longed-for possibility. Similarly, there are agnosticisms and agnosticisms: from a narrowly-conceived scientific naturalism or positivism through a Santayana-like aesthetic experience of the world to a tragic humanism that yearns for ultimate meaning but finds only absurdity and suffering. It is vital to get clear with ourselves just what alternative ways of interpreting and dealing with the world constitute our own struggle, our own real and living option. Such self-clarification is in fact one of the demands of reason upon us.

A genuine option is forced rather than avoidable. There are all sorts and degrees of choices in life and knowledge. There are many choices we can safely avoid; some we positively ought to avoid. The fallacy of the false dilemma is an option often presented to us, and of course we ought steadfastly to resist choosing between its hypotheses. But a forced option is one I cannot avoid making a choice about. As James says, there is "no possibility of not choosing." (15) He will later clarify this matter of "not choosing" by arguing that the Clifford or the Huxley who tells us not to decide regarding religious hypotheses, to leave the matter agnostically open, is in fact urging upon us a certain choice. Faced with a forced option, not to decide may be to decide on one side of the issue. Again, we must remember too that what is a forced option for one person may be an easily avoidable one for another, and vice versa. James persistently poses the issues in existential terms, or as he would say, in terms of our "willing nature."

The momentousness of an option belongs closely together with its forcing itself upon a person. James defines an option as *trivial* "when the opportunity is not unique, when the stake is insignificant, or when the decision is reversible if it later prove unwise." (15) Science, he maintains, is full of trivial options, when nothing is lost by suspending judgment and going back to the laboratory the next day. But of course James would surely not have denied that science also contains its singular, dramatic moments when the stakes are high and a new scientific paradigm is in the balance: Galileo before the Inquisition, Darwin before the scientific defenders of the biblical creation story, or Freud before late-nineteenth-century psychologists. Precisely what makes the challenge of a Galileo, a Darwin, or a Freud so momentous is that their new paradigms dramatically affect our primary beliefs about the world and ourselves; they affect our ethical, metaphysical, and religious views. When options are genuine ones our very selves are in the balance. In ways both subtle and decisive we are "betting our lives" on the truth of one over against other life- and world-perspectives.

At the risk of repetitiousness, I believe it is important to grasp the astonishing practical pluralism of what count as genuine options even and perhaps especially among the well-educated and reflective. By the way he sets up the problem James never lets us off the personal and socio-cultural hook in dealing with our primarily beliefs. Indeed, his analysis of the concrete nature of our moral, metaphysical, and religious struggles and choices is particularly illuminating for those of us who spend our time in academic and liberal-religious environments, were subjective needs and preferences are often masked by a self-deceptive appeal to reason and objectivity. To recognize, scrutinize, and correct for our personal inclinations and beliefs and our cultural biases belongs to the very essence and obligation of rational inquiry. To ignore and pretend that we do not have them is one of its perversions. And when we are honest with one another and ourselves about what hypotheses are live ones for us and what the genuine options for our lives are, we perform an essential human task of self-understanding and self-clarification, one that must be perpetually renewed throughout a lifetime.

In the process we also discover the extraordinarily rich diversity among us on matters of our most basic beliefs and choices. The meanings persons seek and find in life, the values and things to which they attach themselves, the commitments they undertake, the primary or ultimate beliefs they hold--all these are profoundly shaped by the sorts of (developing) persons they are in their concrete socio-cultural contexts. Beliefs that are formally alike as to propositional content can function healthily or neurotically, open persons to transformation into greater good (to speak after the manner of Henry Nelson Wieman) or shut them up and cripple them. I know a spectrum of sensitive, knowledgeable, humane persons who have been opened up to creative transformation through liberal and orthodox Christianity, Judaism, Zen, neo-paganism, various forms of "therapeutic faith," and agnostic humanism. If you ask me which among these persons are the most "rational" in the ways they try to consider things and direct their lives, I do not believe my answer would have any essential relationship to what constitutes their primary beliefs.

Having looked at the three factors involved in what James calls genuine options, I want now to add certain critical qualifications. In his overriding concern to critique scientific reductionism James narrowly identified "agnosticism" with just such reductionism. In fairness to James, it must be said that scientific positivism was a dominant element in the intellectual *Zeitgeist* of his time, and "agnosticism," which T. H. Huxley coined in 1869, was a term closely associated with the scientific approach to things. But in Victorian England--as well as in the U. S.--there were also the great representatives of what I would call an "anguished humanistic agnosticism" such as the George Eliots and the Arthur Hugh Cloughs of the day. Their spiritual agonies over their own inability to believe and their religious nostalgia regarding the general decline of faith must be set side by side with the brisk, cheerful, self-confident agnosticism of W. K. Clifford. Even Huxley was much more tentative and open-minded than James gave him credit for being. As I said earlier, there are--and were--agnosticism and agnosticisms.

Indeed, it is this profoundly existential agnosticism which has been the religiously significant agnosticism of our time: those persons who may have deeply religious longings and who cherish and actively embody humane values, but whose knowledge of the world and personal integrity will not permit them positively to affirm transcendent reality or ultimate meaning. They seem to be solidly represented within liberal religion as well as outside it.

I must add that even with regard to the Huxleys and the Cliffords of his day, I'm not at all sure that James fully appreciated what they were combatting and what they were standing for in their generation. They were conscientious inquirers into what has been called the "ethics of belief" and described so well by Van Harvey in his book *The Historian and the Believer.*[10] Insofar as they were seeking with integrity to carry forward the Enlightenment principle nicely summed up by David Hume's statement that "the wise man proportions his belief to the evidence," they were standing for a principle dear to the heart of liberal religion as well as secular skepticism, and in the teeth of the *Aberglaube* and Know-Nothingism that dominated the religious climate of their day.

It is the recognition that skepticism is a wider and more diverse phenomenon than James described that also requires looking from a slightly different angle at the forced and momentous aspects of living options. The anguished religiously-inclined agnostic knows full well that the alternatives before her or him are momentous ones. She or he knows that a choice is demanded but (sometime in great and enduring agony of spirit) simply cannot make the choice. Between whatever forms of overarching meaning-interpretation and whatever varieties of naturalism constitute her or his concrete options, the anguished agnostic remains suspended and torn. Strictly speaking, James's insistence that suspending judgment agnostically is a practical atheism or naturalism is correct. But because it assumes a somewhat oversimplified account of skepticism it fails to appreciate what can actually be the exquisite spiritual suffering of knowing that even though it is a forced and momentous option one is unable to make it. To call that a "practical atheism" is in one sense true, and in another sense quite inadequate.

---

[10](New York: Macmillan, 1966).

Chapter 7

Indwelling and Exile: Two Types of Religious and Secular World-Orientation

A view that is still widely held tends to identify Christian interpretations of life with other-worldliness, while regarding secular perspectives as straightforwardly this-worldly. Informed participants in and observers of religious life know that "other-worldliness" is a vast oversimplification of the richly dialectical reality of mature religion. They are less likely, however, to question the general assessment of the undialectical this-worldliness of secular philosophies, ideologies, and patterns of life. On the other hand, external students and critics of Christianity who appreciate its world-affirming elements often assume that there is a general correlation between orthodox or conservative forms of Christianity and a higher degree of other-worldliness, and between liberal forms of Christianity and greater world-affirmation.

In this essay I want to suggest and explore a typology which more adequately illuminates both Christian and secular forms of world-orientation. It is a typology of basic determinative psychological styles or ways of being in the world. My selection of the two types I want to present is primarily heuristic. As phenomenological and psychological literature richly shows, there are a number of useful approaches to the complex reality of human being that have brought to light a variety of structural characteristics. At the same time, I believe that organizing

82

human world-orientation around the two poles I do has important implications for our understanding of the relationships between faith and skepticism.[1]

The two types I want to delineate are what I call *indwelling* and *exile*, or "*at home*" and "*not at home*" in the world. The more common terms with which I began--"other-worldly" and "this-worldly"--are limited, somewhat misleading, and finally unsatisfactory ways of trying to talk about these two basic orientations to life, as the ensuing discussion will indicate. Beginning with a description of the two types, I shall spend the rest of the essay illustrating my main point: that these two psychological styles transcend the division between Christian and secular world-orientations. Both sensibilities manifest themselves in Christian and secular ideas and patterns of life alike, and help shed light on the familiar fact that some "believers" seem to have more in common with "unbelievers" than with some of their co-religionists.

Two prefatory comments are necessary here. The first is the usual but important *caveat* about the limitations of typological studies. The very great usefulness of typologies is in helping us conceptually organize and illuminate our experience. But types are of course abstractions, ideal conceptual forms. We seldom find a concrete example which purely incarnates a type; real life is always a "mixed bag." In the context of the present investigation, I intend the two types of world-orientation to point to two contrasting sorts of *governing tendencies* or *emphases* in human personality which shape and manifest themselves in people's ways of relating to and interpreting the world. That we characteristically find the two poles mixed together, Yang/Yin-like, in real human beings should not surprise us.

The second prefatory statement is a substantive one, with what seem to me to be significant theological and philosophical implications: The two types of world-orientation are largely expressions of temperament.[2] When I speak of temperament I have in mind that cluster of dominant psychological dispositions that

---

[1]An issue with which I have been concerned for some time. See, e.g., the Introduction to my book *Borderland Christianity: Critical Reason and the Christian Vision of Love* (Nashville: Abingdon, 1973), 13-13; and my article "Between Faith and Skepticism: A Case Study," *American Journal of Theology and Philosophy*, 1:1, 1980, 1-13.

[2]I explore the role of temperament in theological viewpoints in Chapter 8, "The Personal Dimension in Theological Inquiry."

are the dynamic product in each of us of the finally baffling interplay of our nature, nurture, and circumstances. This is not a case for determinism or a denial of intellectual freedom, but simply a realistic observation of the powerful role of our basic personality traits in shaping our patterns of life and outlooks on the world. I suggest that it is usually the case that we are drawn to a particular way of thinking about or imaging life because it resonates with, articulates, and confirms our own deepest inclinations. To be sure, the processes of existential-intellectual assimilation and rejection are subtle and dialectical. We are corrigible, sometimes surprising, never-fully-transparent, and always-unfinished creatures. Nonetheless, when we are dealing with such fundamental human postures as being "at home" and "not at home" in the world, I believe that a careful analysis of actual people (including of course ourselves) will indicate that temperamental predisposition plays an important role. With the exceptions of pragmatism, existentialism, and personal-narrative modes of reflection, philosophy and theology have still not attended to this personal dimension in our "metaphysical" thinking with the attention I think it deserves--albeit for obvious reasons in the face of its exasperating and slippery "subjectivity."

To turn now to a characterization of the two types: The very terms "indwelling" or "at home" and "exile" or "not at home" are almost self-descriptive in their evocations and connotations. Persons who are at home or "rooted" in the world are those who feel that they really *belong* in the world. Such persons possess a basic sense of harmony with their social and physical environments as their "natural" habitat. "At home" people are inclined to be at least soberly optimistic about the world's possibilities, confident in their own earthly powers, and involved in the practical affairs of the society around them with a robust eagerness. All this is entirely compatible with (although it also may lack) a deep sense of the unfinality and transiency of the world and the limitations and tragedies of human life. Nor are longings for and dreams of the never-more and the might-be necessarily absent. It is just that "indwelling" persons do not "dwell-on" these things. If they take them seriously into account, they do so and then get on with the business of doing what they can while they can. Thus they are inclined to be unsentimental about life and fully "present" in and to it.

By contrast, the person who is "not at home" in the world is characterized by a keen sense of *estrangement* from, of incongruity with, his or her environment.

The world's exiles tend to be afflicted and at times overwhelmed by doubt, pessimism, *Angst*, and despair over the earth and the human situation. They are usually possessed of a heightened--sometimes an excruciating--sensitivity to the ephemerality, fragility, and pain of life. Those for whom the world does not feel like home are restless with the nostalgia of which religion and literature are full: inexpressible longings for long ago and far away, golden ages and celestial cities, ultimate perfection and fulfillment. Exiles may be quite active in the world (although they also may not): striving affirmatively and energetically for earthly goals, capable of quite practical calculation and execution. But at the core of their being gnaws the worm of alienation and pathos which ever and again produces a dyspeptic sense of worldly futility.

Here is a little chart which quickly summarizes these general descriptions of the polar emphases of the two types in their orientations to the world:

Indwelling	*Exile*
belonging	estrangement
harmony	incongruity
optimism	pessimism
confidence	uneasiness
present-ness	nostalgia

Now I want to turn to some modern examples of the two types, again asking the reader to keep in mind that we will not find pure representatives but rather mixtures with one element or the other predominating. Central to my purpose, as I have said, will be to illustrate that the two types of world-orientation are to be found along the spectrum of both Christian and secular outlooks. Naturally in what follows I shall be focussing on articulate expressions of indwelling and exile: well-known persons who have wittingly or unwittingly revealed much about themselves and their views of life in their writings. It should go without saying, however, that the two types of world-orientation are played out daily by all sorts and conditions of human beings--high and low, ordinary and extraordinary, reflective and unreflective. Indeed, if the typology I am exploring is at all useful, an important aspect of its usefulness will be to illuminate not only our theologies and philosophies but more broadly and basically ourselves and the people and social currents around us.

1. "Indwelling" and "exile" as Christian sensibilities

To feel an exile in the world--a "stranger and pilgrim" as the New Testament Letter to the Hebrews has it--is the stereotypical Christian sensibility. Texts seeming to ground and support such an attitude are abundant throughout Christian literature from the beginnings to the present. In a variety of metaphysical ways "exiled" forms of Christian world-orientation are connected with the distinction between this created order and its creative Ground, Context, and Goal. Contrasted with the transcendent realm the world is seen--not without a certain obvious and persuasive "logic"--as inferior, relativized, temporary, and fallen. It is a river to get across, a vale of tears and soul-making, a testing-ground for eternity. The world is the realm mysteriously held captive to Satan, the sphere of deep bondage as well as of radical contingency.

Examples of world-estrangement abound in popular Christian piety, both Catholic and Protestant, down to the present time. Among well-known modern Christian thinkers and writers Søren Kierkegaard provides a good reflective illustration. Although his writings contain abundant evidence of spirited, sensitive immersion in the actualities of daily and cultural life and a richly affirmative aesthetic sensibility, at bottom there is the persistent melancholy and the longing for eternal peace with God. After his strikingly world-affirming characterization of the "knight of faith" early in his writing career,[3] Kierkegaard's central theme of the God-created and -destined "infinity" of the human self combined with his experience of popular ridicule and his reading of the New Testament in his later years to produce the conviction that authentic Christian existence in this fallen world inescapably takes the form of suffering.[4] Only in that eternal fellowship with God for which the human self is created will it find the fulfillment of its confused and restless longings and thus become what it truly is. Only in that eternal home will Christ's victory over sin and death be fully realized and the suffering of the Christian for his sake be justified and transfigured.

---

[3]Søren Kierkegaard, *Fear and Trembling*, translated, with an introduction and notes, by Walter Lowrie (Princeton: Princeton University Press, 1974), 49-51.

[4]See, e.g., *Gospel of Suffering*, translated by A. S. Aldworth and W. S. Ferrie (London: James Clarke & Co., Ltd., 1955); and *The Last Years: Journals 1853-1855*, edited and translated by Ronald Gregor Smith (London: Collins, 1965).

Prominent examples of Christian world-skepticism exist in contemporary Christianity as well. The novels of Graham Greene are permeated by an Augustinian Catholic pessimism about human motives and possibilities, with heavily ironic, mock-heroic, ambiguity-riddled deaths as their characteristic climax.[5] Sharing the subtlety of Greene's world-pessimism (but lacking his fine sense of ironic humor) was Simone Weil, the mystic and unbaptized Roman Catholic convert who is surely one of the most unusual and provocative Christians of this century. When all due qualifications have been made in the light of her powerful affirmations of the created order and our concrete fellowship with one another as common citizens of the "universal city," pervading Weil's writings is an "exilic" mentality which is closely related to the solitariness and suffering in her own life.[6] In the case of Weil it is necessary to look behind the content of her world-affirmative remarks to the austere language of suffering and estrangement with which they are surrounded. An even more explicit and intense pessimism bordering on the Manichaean undergirds the religious and autobiographical writings of journalist and critic Malcolm Muggeridge. Muggeridge uses his acerbic wit and keen powers of observation relentlessly to expose the utter bondage and futility of all human and earthly enterprises. The divine grace primarily saves us wretched sinners *out* of this world in which all is vanity.[7]

Among most contemporary Christian theologians and writers, however, it is considered absolutely *de rigueur* to be robustly "at home" in the world. Children of modern secularization, inheritors of the modern biblical and theological discovery of the world-affirmation of Israel's faith, disciples of Dietrich Bonhoeffer and other theological analysts and affirmers of secularization, participants in the upheavals of the twentieth century and students of the classical Marxist critique of religion's "other-worldliness," we have fallen all over ourselves in our eagerness to be, and to be seen to be, just as *bona fide* "indwellers" as our secular comrades.

But for all that, most modern theologians have remained at least formally dialectical in retaining the classical Christian hope that looks beyond this world for

---

[5]Just three examples out of several are *The Power and the Glory, The End of the Affair*, and *A Burnt-out Case* (all available in 1977 Penguin editions).

[6]See her *Waiting for God*, translated by Emma Craufurd, with an Introduction by Leslie A. Fiedler (N. Y.: Harper & Row, 1973); especially her letters and the essay "The Love of God and Affliction."

[7]See, e.g., *Jesus Rediscovered* (New York: Doubleday, 1979).

ultimate fulfillment, while interpreting the content of that hope with an appropriately "agnostic" modesty and reserve and focussing on this world and its possibilities. One of the many misunderstandings during the early years of Bonhoeffer interpretation was the failure to appreciate that the "non-religious interpretation" of the prison letters was a new way of talking about the fully dialectical reality of Christian faith, *not* a theological reductionism.[8] The man who wrote of a new kind of "worldly" holiness, who preferred to speak of God "at the center of life" and not at all at its boundaries was also the one who could write in very traditional language of the eternal God and the assurance that all things were embraced within the redemptive purpose of God in Christ.[9]

At the beginning of this essay I said that "this-worldliness" and "other-worldliness" were too limited and misleading to use as general terms to characterize the two modes of world-orientation I am trying to describe and illustrate. My portrayal of contemporary theological "at-home-ness" in terms of its relationship to the traditional Christian hope of eternal life is essential to the discussion of "indwelling" and "exile" as religious attitudes, but may be similarly misleading. The crucial point to clarify here is that while most Christian forms of the "exiled" sensibility affirm eternal life with God as the ultimate goal and reality of human existence, the statement is not convertible. Affirmation of eternal life does not in itself express an "exiled" frame of mind. In the case of any Christian believer and writer we must look not simply at the "what" of her or his views on the kingdom of God but much more at the "how" of her or his total evaluation--both cognitive and affective--of the world. The pages of *Letters and Papers from Prison* are striking in their robust and vigorous love of life and the world and their sharp criticisms of forms of Christian faith that emphasize "inwardness," suffering, and other-worldliness. Equally striking in that context, however, is their repeated affirmation

---

[8]Numerous Bonhoeffer interpreters have noted this and sought to correct it in their own expositions of Bonhoeffer. A central theme of my own study of Bonhoeffer was the dialectical coherence between the ideas in the prison writings and his earlier thought: see *Bonhoeffer's Theology: Classical and Revolutionary* (New York and Nashville: Abingdon Press, 1970), especially "Paths in Bonhoeffer Interpretation," 279-302.

[9]Dietrich Bonhoeffer, *Letters and Papers from Prison*, The Enlarged Edition, edited by Eberhard Bethge, translated by Reginald Ruller, Frank Clarke and others with additional material translated by John Bowden (New York: Macmillan, 1972), 376, 391, 393.

of what Bonhoeffer called the "full content" of Christian doctrine, including the hope of eternal life.[10]

Just as the affirmation of eternal life is compatible with both an "exilic" and an "indwelling" world-orientation, so likewise are Christian orthodoxy and liberalism together with the various shadings in between. G. K. Chesterton and C. S. Lewis must both be regarded as robustly orthodox Christians; both were also robustly world-affirming persons.[11] Karl Barth's creative "neo-orthodox" interpretation of Christianity, with its vigorous reaffirmation of the doctrines of original sin and divine grace and sovereignty, went hand in hand with a joyous lust for life and earthy "at-home-ness" in the world.[12] By contrast, Albert Schweitzer, who early on came to a radically liberal view of Jesus and Christianity and ended his life a self-described humanist, was deeply haunted and at times almost overcome throughout his life by the suffering caused by a ceaseless competition of life with life in nature.[13] Interestingly, on the specific issue of life after death, perhaps no contemporary theologian has written more on, or seemed more preoccupied with, the subject than the British philosopher-theologian John Hick, who by almost any criterion must be seen as a liberal in his interpretation of the Christian message and its relationship to other religious truth-claims.[14] Not that

---

[10]See, e.g., Bonhoeffer's critical remarks on Bultmann's demythologizing project: *Letters and Papers*, 285-287, 327-329.

[11]The Chesterton of the Father Brown detective series is surely a man fascinatedly "at home" in the world: see *The Father Brown Omnibus* (New York: Dodd, 1983); but the same spirit is there in his best-known theological work, *Orthodoxy* (London: The Bodley Head, 1908). Lewis, who was influenced by Chesterton, also combined a "high" and unabashed supernaturalism with a crisp, no-nonsense immersion in the world around him and (also like Chesterton) a sheer delight in the aesthetic. This is especially apparent in his beloved *Narnia Chronicles* (all available from Collier Books) and his literary essays, but it permeates his theological works as well; see, e.g., *The Four Loves* (New York: Harcourt Brace Jovanovich, 1960) and *Mere Christianity* (London: Collins, 1952).

[12]See Eberhard Busch's definitive biography, *Karl Barth: His Life from Letters and Autobiographical Texts*, translated by John Bowden (Philadelphia: Fortress Press, 1976).

[13]His autobiography, *Out of My Life and Thought*, reveals this lifelong anguish and brooding sense of dis-ease in the world (translated by C. T. Campion, New York: Henry Holt and Company, 1933).

[14]On his liberal Christianity, see Hick's *Christianity at the Centre* (London: SCM Press Ltd., 1968); and *God Has Many Names* (Philadelphia: Westminster Press, 1982). The Christian hope of eternal life is central to Hick's analysis of the truth-claims of Christianity, expressed in the concept of "eschatological

Hick exhibits an "exilic" mentality thereby; he is simply a modern Christian thinker who believes that it is essential to the "logic" of the faith fully to affirm the hope of eternal life. Again, my point is that we must look at the full content, and more deeply still, at the tone of theological writings and set completely aside all *a priori* notions or superficial expectations. My discussion of Christian liberalism and orthodoxy further illustrates, I believe, that a typology of "indwelling" and "exile" is more illuminating in getting at root patterns of world-orientation in Christian thought and life.

2. Secular forms of "indwelling" and "exile"

If the sense of exile is the stereotypically Christian attitude toward the world, the feeling of "at-home-ness" is the stereotypically secular frame of mind. Historically the modern roots of this secular sensibility are foreshadowed in the Renaissance and emerge with vigor and explicitness in the eighteenth-century Enlightenment, beginning that decisive turn toward fascinated immersion in this world of human institutions, ideas, and consciousness that has dominated and defined what we call the modern world. Modern Enlightenment-inspired "indwelling" has been marked by an optimism of which two chief expressions have been the beliefs in historical progress and in human perfectibility. Its characteristic metaphysics has been a naturalism which--perhaps paradoxically--interprets the human race both entirely as the product and indweller of nature and at the same time as the rational controller of nature.

Illustrations of this secular sense of harmony with the world are of course abundant and hardly need dwelling on. The French *philosophes* of the eighteenth century, notably Diderot and Condorcet, are the great early modern exemplars, with their call for the liberation of humankind through reason from the shackles of a superstitious other-worldliness and for the building of paradise on earth.[15] For all his sobriety regarding human nature and his decisive critique of Enlightenment

---

verification" which he has expounded in several articles and books; see, e.g., "Eschatological Verification Reconsidered," *Religious Studies* 13:2, June 1977, 189-202. His chief work on the problem of eternal life is *Death and Eternal Life* (New York: Harper & Row, 1976).

[15] See, e.g., Condorcet's *Outline of the Progress of the Human Mind*, a work which rather remarkably prophesies certain later developments such as various technological advances and the movement for the equality of the sexes.

thought, Immanuel Kant was likewise dominated by Enlightenment faith in human autonomy and its utopian possibilities.[16]

If the eighteenth century proclaimed the gospel of full world-affirmation, many dominant voices of the nineteenth century believed it was being increasingly actualized in their time. The period from about 1850 to 1914 was indeed a "golden age" of European culture, when the forces of oppression and ignorance, disease and war seemed to be yielding on every hand to the march of science, democratic institutions, and education.[17] The feelings of optimism and earthly self-confidence accompanying this rather remarkable era of the *Pax Britannica* widely permeated both secular and religious thought. Among secular thinkers and writers we find it in social theoreticians like Marx and Engels, in philosophers like Herbert Spencer, in scientists like T. H. Huxley, and in poets like Algernon Charles Swinburne.

In characterizing the "indwelling" sensibility earlier in this essay, I said that it is quite compatible with sensitivity to the transiency, the tragedies, and the psychosocial distortions of human life. While many forms of eighteenth- and nineteenth-century secular (and also religious) world-affirmation are in retrospect fatuously optimistic, not all are; in very different ways Voltaire, John Stuart Mill, and Friedrich Nietzsche were clear-eyed critics of the illusions of their time.[18] After Verdun and Hiroshima, Auschwitz and the Gulag, no twentieth-century versions of "at-home-ness" can be taken seriously that do not stare these horrors and their implications squarely in the face. It should hardly need saying that most forms of contemporary humanism and naturalism have thoroughly rejected the superficial optimism dominating eighteenth- and nineteenth-century secular thought; yet a lingering Christian stereotype of secular world-views still tends to bind them

---

[16]See, e.g., his "Idea for a Universal History with a Cosmopolitan Intent" in Immanuel Kant, *Perpetual Peace and Other Essays*, translated, with Introduction, by Ted Humphrey (Indianapolis: Hackett Publishing Company, 1983).

[17]Will Herberg portrayed in capsule form the European world in 1912, contrasting it sharply with the post-World War II world, in *Judaism and Modern Man* (New York: Harper & Row, 1951), 3-6.

[18]Voltaire was, of course, in his classic satire *Candide* (translated by Lowell Bair, New York: Bantam Books, 1981); Mill in such works as *Three Essays on Religion* (New York: Greenwood Press; reprint of 1874 edition) and *The Subjection of Women* (London: D. Appleton, 1869); and Nietzsche throughout his works. A good compendium of central Nietzschean themes is *Twilight of the Idols*, translated, with an Introduction and Commentary, by R. J. Hollingdale, (Harmondsworth, England: Penguin Books Ltd.), 1968.

to their Enlightenment past and thereby to set up an easy "straw man" for criticism.

Not that there are no contemporary examples around of an only somewhat chastened Enlightenment-style optimism about the human situation and prospect. Significantly, all the versions of this sort of humanism of which I can think are to be found in the United States, the country more than any other in which eighteenth-century faith in human nature and historical progress became integral to its national ideology and in which the faith still survives at both a popular and a sophisticated level. These recent expressions of a kind of Rousseauistic "indwelling" are all variations on the technocratic mentality. Through the proper sorts of social and technological tinkering the many ills besetting us can be alleviated if not simply resolved, and we can look forward to a future bright with widespread prosperity and peace if we will only apply our rapidly advancing knowledge and techniques. Herman Kahn of the Rand Corporation is perhaps the best-known representative of this optimism.[19] Another well-known exponent is B. F. Skinner, who characteristically combines a scientific naturalism and determinism with a cheerful utilitarian confidence in the possibilities of redesigning the human environment so that people will be generally happier.[20]

But what the typology of "indwelling" and "exile" as basic dispositional emphases in both Christian and secular world-orientations illuminates for us is the counter-stereotypical fact that there is a contemporary secular sensibility at the opposite pole from Skinner and Kahn: a profoundly tragic sense of life, an intense perception of the depths of human bondage and the indifference of nature without the consolation of redemption here or hereafter, a feeling of the ultimate futility and forlornness of the human condition. Nor is this secular sensibility simply the product of our own appalling century, although it has certainly achieved its most widespread forms of expression over the past seventy years. In the nineteenth century, even Mark Twain's comedies contain much incisive and sometimes bitter satire of human folly; and such works as *The Mysterious Stranger* and *Letters from the Earth* are darkly and unrelievedly pessimistic about the human race and its place

---

[19]Herman Kahn, *The Coming Boom: Economic, Political, Social* (New York: Simon & Schuster, 1983).

[20]See, e.g, his *Walden Two* (New York: Macmillan, 1976 reissue); and *Beyond Freedom and Dignity* (New York: Bantam, 1971), especially chapters 8 and 9. In fairness, Skinner has become more cautionary and tentative, as in his Introduction to the above reissue of *Walden Two*, "Walden Two Revisited."

in the scheme of things.[21]

But it is the twentieth century--primarily and significantly in Europe--that has produced whole schools of thought and art expressive of a view of human situation as radically godless, homeless, meaningless, and hopeless. The paradigm word is "absurdity," and it has manifested itself in central aspects of such artistic movements as Dadaism and the theatre of the absurd.[22] Samuel Beckett's bleak and desperate human landscapes in such plays as *Waiting for Godot* are perhaps the best-known and most striking articulations of this "exilic" mentality.[23]

Atheistic forms of existentialist thought in certain of their moods and some of their themes and language have tended toward a world-orientation emphasizing human "abandonment" and despair, and of course that has certainly been the popular caricature of existentialism. The young Albert Camus in *The Myth of Sisyphus* relentlessly developed the "logic of absurdity" in such directions, and Jean-Paul Sartre seemed almost to relish speaking of human reality as a "useless passion."[24] Yet humanistic existentialism is not in the fullness of its articulation a philosophy of exile but a call to world-affirmation through creativity, community, and ethical and political action. For all of its sometimes dramatic metaphors of human estrangement in the world, even Camus's *Sisyphus* is in the last analysis a celebration of the uniqueness and creative possibilities of human life; and his later works, while grimly and acutely preoccupied with the horrors of the twentieth century, also argue eloquently for the enduring character of values wrested out of our human relationship to one another and the world. In his famous lecture "Existentialism is Humanism," Sartre replied effectively to the popular criticism of

---

[21]Mark Twain, *The Mysterious Stranger and Other Stories* (New York: New American Library, 1962); and *Letters from the Earth* (New York: Harper & Row, 1974).

[22]See, e.g., the remarks of Tristan Tzara, "Dadaism," in Richard Ellmann and Charles Feidelson, Jr., eds., *The Modern Tradition: Backgrounds of Modern Literature* (New York: Oxford University Press, 1965), 595-601.

[23]Samuel Beckett, *Waiting for Godot* (New York: Grove Press, 1954).

[24]Albert Camus, *The Myth of Sisyphus and Other Essays*, translated by Justin O'Brien (New York: Random House, 1955); Jean-Paul Sartre, *Being and Nothingness: An Essay in Phenomenological Ontology*, translated and with an Introduction by Hazel E. Barnes (New York: Philosophical Library, 1956).

existentialist philosophies as pessimistic and set forth in stirring brevity his radical affirmation of human freedom and responsibility.25

Viewed in the full range of their themes, secular forms of existentialist thought such as we find in Camus and Sartre are examples of what we might call "mainstream" contemporary humanism. I have previously indicated that "mainstream" contemporary Christian thought, whether conservative or liberal, is profoundly dialectical in holding together an "indwelling" world-orientation and the historic hope of eternal life. I want now to suggest that "mainstream" secular perspectives have their own dialectic: the full affirmation of life in this world as our proper and only human habitation, together with the full and sensitive recognition of the depth of human bondage and suffering and an accompanying refusal to deify humanity or the world. The one dialectic believes that our ultimate context is beyond this present world, while affirming life here and now as good and as absolutely integral to that larger context. The other rejects any human context other than this world, but realistically faces the implications of that world-view given the negative conditions of life and refuses to make virtue of necessity by an idolatrous devotion to nature, society, or the individual.

The mature Camus of *The Plague, The Rebel*, and the post-war essays seems to me an outstanding exemplar of the "dialectical" humanism of which I have been speaking.26 He was one of the most clear-sighted and unflinching unmaskers of the peculiar crimes and tragedies of the twentieth century and the enduring ills of the human condition. At the same time, he celebrated with a passionate lyricism the natural "graces" in human life in every age: above all beauty, compassion, and the word of truth. He sought to illuminate permanent values brought to light precisely through the human experience of revolt against oppressions of every sort: human life itself, human community, justice, moderation and limits in human action. Camus was an unrelenting foe of modern ideologies which dethrone God only to put an absolutist vision of humanity in God's place, and traced the fateful course by

---

25"Existentialism is a Humanism," in Walter Kaufmann, ed., *Existentialism from Doestoevsky to Sartre* (New York: New American Library, 1975), 345-369.

26Albert Camus, *The Plague*, translated by Stuart Gilbert (New York: Modern Library, 1948); *The Rebel*, translated by Anthony Bower with a Foreword by Sir Herbert Read (New York: Random House, 1956); *Lyrical and Critical Essays*, translated by Ellen Conroy Kennedy, edited and with notes by Philip Thody (New York: Alfred A. Knopf, 1968).

which the authentic revel so often becomes the revolutionary ideologue. Deeply aware of human finitude, he affirmed our inextricable relationship with the natural world and would not join in those various modern tendencies completely to historicize human existence. As he wrote in *The Rebel*: ". . . the only original rule of life today [is] to learn to live and to die, and, in order to be a man, to refuse to be a god."[27]

I could of course cite a number of other distinguished twentieth-century secular thinkers who likewise embody in richly varied ways what I have called a dialectical affirmation of human "at-home-ness" in the world. To mention only a few: Sigmund Freud, Bertrand Russell, and Martin Heidegger as important intellectual and moral influences of the century; and in our own day humanists such as Andrei Sakharov and Michael Harrington.[28] Their writings further illustrate a "mainstream" humanism which exhibits a fully "indwelling" secular world-orientation while facing honestly all the problems and implications of such a view given the realities of human life in the world.

3. Conclusion

In this essay I have sought to show that a phenomenology of "styles" of world-orientation--what I have called the types of "indwelling" and "exile"--enables us to transcend the usual stereotypes regarding both Christian and secular forms of world-orientation and look at them in their actual complexity with fresh eyes. I trust that I have shown that the still-typical categorizations in terms of other-worldliness/this-worldliness and (within Christian thought, although one could have show a similar phenomenon in secular thought) relationship between world-orientation and liberal/conservative views, are inadequate, inaccurate, and misleading. There are Christian writers who do indeed seem to be "other-worldly" in their outlook; but the evidence of other Christian thinkers who are robustly "this-worldly" makes it clear that the issue hangs, not on belief in or rejection of the hope of eternal life or on being "liberal" or "orthodox," but on what I have called "indwelling" and "exilic" sensibilities which interpret Christian faith accordingly.

---

[27]*The Rebel*, 306.

[28]See Andrei Sakharov, *Alarm and Hope* (New York: Random House, 1978); and Michael Harrington, *The Politics at God's Funeral: The Spiritual Crisis of Western Civilization* (New York: Viking Penguin Inc., 1983).

Among humanists we predictably find those who are vigorously and optimistically "this-worldly," but we also find deep-dyed pessimists; while the "mainstream" secular sensibility is a dialectical world-orientation characterized by both affirmation and realism. Again, these differences among secular writers are illuminated better in terms of the mentalities of "at-home-ness" and "not-at-home-ness" than by division along theoretical or ideological lines.

At the beginning of my essay I said that organizing human world-orientation around the two poles of "indwelling" and "exile" has important implications for our understanding of the relationships between faith and skepticism. I went on to state my thesis that the two dispositional styles transcend the division between Christian and secular world-orientations. It should be apparent by now what I had in mind in making these statements. By focussing on basic sensibilities rather than simply on intellectual content in Christian and secular world-views, we realize that there are "kinship lines" running across the two such that a Christian may have more in common with a humanist in his or her deepest responses to life and on a number of issues than with a fellow Christian--and vice versa. There are Christians of an "exilic" mentality who rejoice in and welcome every manifestation of pessimism and even nihilism from humanist quarters. It has been a standard homiletical device of some well-known fundamentalist evangelists, although it was also fashionable, I recall, among some "neo-orthodox" scholars, clergy, and seminarians of my own theological generation of some thirty years ago. By contrast, a Dietrich Bonhoeffer working in the German resistance movement during World War II identified much more closely with his secular comrades-in-conspiracy, who risked their lives for purely human values and hopes, than he did with many other Christians.[29] Bonhoeffer's experience has been confirmed repeatedly by many Christians since then, especially in connection with social and political concerns.

To say that a person is a "believer" or a "skeptic," a Christian or a secular humanist, is to say very little. It is in fact completely uninformative until we begin to delineate first the content of one's religious faith or secular outlook (and the range here is vast within both Christianity and humanism), and then at a still more deeply "existential" level to discern the personal and largely dispositional world-

---

[29]See, e.g., *Letters and Papers*, 200, 281-282, 325-327, 344-346.

orientation underlying it. In this task of clarification and understanding I suggest that something like phenomenology of "indwelling" and "exile" can be useful.

Chapter 8

The Personal Dimension in Theological Inquiry

Over the years I have repeatedly observed in my theological colleagues and myself the striking degree to which our different interests, perspectives, and methods reflect our personal character and training. It is a common observation, but I wonder whether we take it with the seriousness it deserves and really pursue its implications. I have pondered the matter a great deal and mentioned it on occasion to colleagues and others, but it seems to be one of those uncomfortable acknowledgements that we tend to suppress in our professional activity and interchange. I suspect that for the most part we simply do not know what to do with the recognition of these seemingly adventitious autobiographical elements in our pursuit of truth. To incorporate them bodily into our reflections appears to carry with it the threat of somehow dissolving the validity of reason in a murky and bottomless subjectivism. It can also, more personally, be deeply disturbing to certain images we have of ourselves and our work both as individuals and as a community of scholars.

Various thinkers have been reminding us of the personal dimensions of our knowledge for many years. William James, who remains America's timeliest and most refreshingly original philosopher, saw with disturbing clarity the largely unacknowledged role of temperament in the history and practice of philosophy and its influence in systems and schools of thought. He coined the typology of "tough-minded" and "tender-minded" philosophers, which illuminates philosophers and their styles as revealingly today as it did in James's nineteenth century.[1] In our time no one has explored the personal dimensions in the pursuit of knowledge as exhaustively as Michael Polanyi. In the following passage he emphasizes the role of individual character and training in rational inquiry:

> I must admit that I can fulfill my obligation to serve the truth only to the extent of my natural ability as developed by my education. No one can transcend his formative milieu very far, and beyond this area he must rely on it uncritically. I consider that this matrix of my thought determines my personal calling. It both offers me my opportunity for seeking the truth and limits my responsibility for arriving at my own conclusions.[2]

Elsewhere Polanyi balanced the "determined" aspects of our knowledge with a robust advocacy of the freedom of the mind within these limitations, but he was deeply concerned to remind us that we never escape them even in the highest reaches of theoretical knowledge.

I could go on to mention the important insights of some of the leading existentialist thinkers into the personal matrix of all our inquiries and its role in shaping these inquiries, but James and Polanyi will serve as representative figures. In this essay I want simply to add my own current reminder, because I believe it is a vitally important, inescapable, and permanent issue. I suggest that in our search for truth in theology and other disciplines we are obliged at minimum consciously to recognize and incorporate as an essential self-critical principle the limitations imposed on each of us by our own character structure and the particular background and education that are intimately bound up with it. Only in this way can we achieve the realism, modesty, openness, and perspective that are demanded by the very notion of a *human* approach to and apprehension of truth. The alternative is self-deception, which ranges from a sometimes amusing obliviousness through a tedious pomposity to an insufferable arrogance.

Differences of "nature and nurture" influence to one degree or another the quest for truth in all communities of intellectual inquiry. A more acute and self-

---

[1]His classic discussion of the two types is in Lecture One of *Pragmatism,* in *Pragmatism and Other Essays* (New York: Washington Square Press, 1963), 5-21.

[2]*Knowing and Being* (Marjorie Grene, ed., Chicago: University of Chicago Press, 1969), 133.

critical awareness of that fact on the part of both scientists and humanists would spare us a great deal of sterile impasse, destructive acrimony, and plain silliness. There is one important sense in which scholars are especially vulnerable to self-deception: We like to think of ourselves as eminently rational, and the rules of the professional games we play with one another demand the maintenance of this self-image despite considerable personal and collegial experience to the contrary. As a result--and of course ironically in seekers of truth--we often cloak personal preferences and prejudices in a mantle of scholarship; we often seem willfully unaware when our reasoning has become rationalization. As James observed in his study of temperament in philosophy: "There arises thus a certain insincerity in our philosophic discussions: the potentest of all our premises is never mentioned."[3] Substantial ignorance of our real motives is a general feature of the human situation, but it is a painful incongruity in those of us who are dedicated to overcoming ignorance. Socrates' "Know thyself" was the disclosure of a vital precondition and constant self-critical principle in the search for truth. It is a dictum which I myself have only begun in the middle of my life and career really to appreciate and appropriate.

There is of course a very good reason for the situation I have described. In every discipline, scholars are trained in knowledge of what is outside or other than the individual self. The epistemologically essential principles of objectivity and universality, and the methods they generate, direct us precisely away from our own merely subjective and particular personalities. This outer-directedness permeates not only the natural sciences but also the behavioral sciences and the humanities. We in the *Geisteswissenschaften* study such phenomena as cultural systems, social stratification, historical epochs, language and literary expression, creative geniuses and their works, learning theory, the problem of freedom and determinism, and the like--not the hardly noticeable individual mind that does the studying.

The necessity and the achievements of rational inquiry in the human quest for knowledge of and a measure of control over ourselves and our environment are indisputable and need no defense. Lest it be thought that I am attempting to dissolve the pursuit of knowledge in the acids of subjectivity, let me here emphatically affirm that enormous body of principles, procedures, and conclusions

---

[3]*Pragmatism and Other Essays*, 7.

the validity of which is quite independent of our personal makeup. The formal validity of reasoning itself, articulated in self-evident and extrapolated logical principles and rules, imposes itself upon us with the force of necessity, sovereignly transcending our individual desires; we deny or ignore it only at the price of self-contradictions and fallacies. Empirical knowledge is of course always contingent and corrigible; inductive reasoning about our experience of the world, with its fruitful but fateful gaps between data and interpretation, premises and conclusions, is understandably a major battleground in our warfare against ignorance and error. And yet there is a very considerable accumulation of theories and hypotheses, methods, and conclusions in both scientific knowledge and everyday life which it is a Pyrrhonic foolishness not to rely upon with confidence. That the Battle of Hastings was fought in England in 1066, that copper conducts electricity, that there are books in my office--these and a host of propositions ranging from the quotidian to the theoretical are entirely independent of autobiographical considerations.

But of course there are also a large number of crucially significant aspects of empirical knowledge, humanistic evaluation, and general world-interpretation about which there is much more disagreement; and it is precisely these important areas in our search for truth which are the most susceptible to personal factors and about which seekers after truth need to become and remain acutely aware. The relative roles of genetic and cultural factors in human behavior is a prime and venerable example from the realm of empirical knowledge, of which the controversy over sociobiology is only the most recent phase. In such paradigmatically humanistic inquiries as literary and arts criticism there is a substantial component of factual knowledge and essential skills; and yet there is notorious lack of agreement regarding both methods and interpretations. One need mention only the historical vicissitudes in interpretation of Dickens and Joyce, Bach and Schoenberg, Picasso and Pollack, to indicate the importance not only of changing fashions and tastes but also of personal predilections in evaluating literature and the arts. Empirical theories of maximum generality and humanistic interpretations of distinctively human activities in turn shade off into metaphysical and theological speculations about the nature of reality, for which empirical knowledge is necessary but far from sufficient. At the interpretative level of a Hegel or a Whitehead, a Barth or a Tillich, subjective factors again have very free play.

Along with a number of other much more eminent thinkers before me, I am simply urging each and all of us to be more keenly aware and to develop some depth understanding of that inescapable foundation and matrix of all our knowledge: our own selves. The very successes of outer-directed inquiry encourage a serious imbalance in the total picture of the knowing situation which needs repeatedly to be rectified by inner-directed attention. Significantly, this enriching and correcting of our knowledge is precisely demanded by the rational goal of comprehensiveness and completeness in the description and explanation of phenomena. Also, of course, the very process of self-knowledge and self-criticism, which importantly involves some natively sensitive self-awareness and common sense, is considerably deepened and clarified by objective knowledge obtained from, say, depth-psychological theories of behavior. Thus acquiring some awareness of the autobiographical material in my quest for truth is entirely consistent with--indeed, demanded by--the presuppositions, methods, and goals of rational inquiry itself.

I have been speaking of the importance of recognizing the personal dimension of intellectual investigation generally. But my readers will surely agree that among the scholarly disciplines theology by its very nature exhibits a high degree of subjectivity. It is by no means unique in this; I have mentioned humanistic interpretation in literary and arts criticism and metaphysical speculation generally, and might have included certain whole modes of doing philosophy such as existentialism. But theology clearly and richly lies at the "existential" end of the knowledge spectrum. For theology is faith seeking understanding: reasoned reflection on the object, meaning, context, and implications of what is at bottom a personal religious commitment. As such it is profoundly and inescapably rooted in subjectivity, and this rooting manifests itself both in the presuppositions and in the style and method of the theologian.

To be sure, the faith of the individual believer stands within a world religious community having common sources and a common tradition along with its great internal diversity. The Christian theologian understands her or his own work within a long history of theological interpretation from the Church Fathers to the present, with the biblical writings as the crystallized normative witness and thus the stable foundation of that ongoing interpretation. The theologian's personal faith and its theological articulation are always oriented beyond mere subjectivity toward the Christian community and its heritage of Bible, creeds, doctrines, ministry, worship, ethics, and theological tradition. All this gives theological inquiry its "objective" dimension, its character as a commonly shared universe of discourse in which genuinely rational discussion and criticism take place.

But unlike the natural-scientific community, any particular world religious community is only one among many and there is no general agreement among them as to assumptions, procedures, and conclusions. This pluralistic situation continues within each religious tradition, with its varied sub-communities making competing claims rightly to interpret the larger tradition. Every tradition and sub-tradition is finally filtered and interpreted through the personal faith of very different individual adherents. Wilfred Cantwell Smith has very usefully reminded us that "religions" are abstractions; that we are closer to reality in speaking of the faith of individual persons sharing a common tradition.[4]

For all the theologian's self-conscious orientation to and awareness of her or his particular religious tradition in its complex wholeness, the *fides quae creditur* is still mediated through the *fides qua*; and she or he brings to both faith and faith-seeking-understanding a particular temperament and life-experience. Some, usually more classical, modes of theologizing have tried to put this personal dimension as much in the background as possible, as for example those that have seen the task of theology simply as explicating church dogmas closely following official guidelines. Others, especially in contemporary theology, have revelled in the personal and the pluralistic and articulated a kind of "artistic" model of theological reflection that places a high value on individual imagination and creativity. But those who prefer the former theological modes and we who read them should not be deceived by the appearance of "high" objectivity. Nietzsche's remarks about philosophical systems are surely applicable to theological systems as well: a chief value of reading them is as unintended portraits of their authors.

The most significant and salutary contribution of the recent autobiographical or narrative approaches to theological inquiry is having made quite explicit this inescapable rootedness of theology in personal experience and attempting to work out some of its implications. One of the finest--and one of the most widely

---

[4]Wilfred Cantwell Smith, *The Meaning and End of Religion* (New York: Harper & Row, 1978).

neglected--theologians writing today is the Anglican priest and religious Harry A. Williams, who through his own travail and dramatic resurrection with the help of psychoanalysis clearly perceived the need for theology explicitly to acknowledge and be informed by its grounding in personal experience and self-understanding. In his provocative early essay "Theology and Self-Awareness" in the 1962 volume *Soundings*, long before the recent autobiographical theologies, he wrote of the essential importance of the Freudian revolution to the task of the theologian:

> Our concern here will be to discover how a man's knowledge of God and his attitude towards God are affected by his growing awareness of what he is and how he functions as a psychic entity. This of course will have important results in his subsequent statement of how any Christian doctrine is to be understood, but this statement of doctrine will be at second remove. . . . Freud and his successors . . .have taught us how we can discover within ourselves a great deal of what was previously unknown to us, and such discoveries can tell us a great deal of how we think and feel about God. But the process is not simply an exercise in cerebration. It involves a costly surrender of what we imagine or hope or fear we are, to what in our fullness we really are. Unless we are prepared for this surrender, the new understanding of human nature which Freud initiated will tell us nothing useful about that belief in God which is the material of our theology. It is only by doing the truth that we come to the light. It is only by actually making the journey that we can perceive the nature of the country. There is a type of thinking which remains safely at home, merely receiving reports, maps, and photographs of what lies beyond the garden wall, and speculates, often with great cleverness, on the basis of such dispatches received. . . . But in such circumstances the object of thought becomes no more than an imaginary toy. That is why so much talk about God cuts no ice. What is talked about has never been lived. . . . The principle of Incarnation, as Christian theology understands it, is the principle of involvement. In Christ, we believe, God involved himself totally in our human predicament. How then, with regard to our own selves and psychic make-up, can we refuse to do the same? And here Freud pointed the way. . . .5

I have thought it worthwhile to quote the somewhat lengthy passage above, because in it Williams sharply reminds us of what we know is true but too seldom bring to light: the decisive hidden relationship between our unconscious desires and conflicts and our faith and theological reflection; and he spends the rest of the essay

---

5A. R. Vidler, ed., *Soundings: Essays Concerning Christian Understanding* (Cambridge: Cambridge University Press, 1962), 72-73.

effectively illustrating the phenomenon in a variety of ways. The passage I have quoted also felicitously locates the demand for self-awareness squarely within the context of the Christian doctrines of Incarnation, "doing the truth," and finding through losing.

In his profound and beautiful book *True Resurrection*, Williams states in the opening sentence that "This book is an attempt to explore my own experience." A little later, looking back on the *Soundings* essay, he remarks, "I have long felt that theological inquiry is basically related to self-awareness and that therefore it involves a process of self-discovery so that, whatever else theology is, it must in some sense be a theology of the self."[6] It is important to make two contextual points about these words. The first is that Williams does not simply reduce theology to a mode of self-reflection, and his books, with their solid grounding in the Christian theological tradition, make this clear. But he *is* saying that all authentic theologizing must be consciously aware of, existentially grounded in, and reflectively congruent with the theologian's own searching self-discovery. The second is that when Williams tells us that he is going to explore his own experience we are not to expect that in what follows he is going to tell us his life story, "spill his guts," or indulge in self-advertisement. One of the striking things about Williams' writings in the light of his announced commitment to a "theology of the self" is how gracefully he transposes his own inner and outer experience into a universally available form. His theological reflection is always intimately related to and permeated by concrete and contemporary examples that are precisely essential to the reflection. It is clear that Williams takes many of these "case studies" from his own life and relationship, and yet they are never cast in a literary form that announces, "Here is Harry Williams talking about himself!" Instead they draw us immediately and persuasively into the human situation itself. When Williams uses the pronoun "I" it is natural and unassuming, drawing attention to the personal authenticity of the reflections rather than to the person of the author.

I have dwelt a bit on the lack of autobiographical story or confession in Williams' writings because I suspect that a common misconception about theologizing that is grounded in self-awareness is that it must take just those literary and methodological forms. Some theologians have on occasion used the personal

---

[6]Harry A. Williams, *True Resurrection* (New York: Harper & Row, 1972), ix.

narrative or confessional modes, and done it very effectively. But no religious thinker uses them exclusively, and they are simply one way--albeit the most explicit way--in which self-consciously to embody the personal rooting of theological reflection. Bringing to conscious awareness the autobiographical grounding and shaping of theological inquiry can express itself in a variety of ways precisely because it is not a specific form and method but a whole mode of theological awareness.

I do not want to underestimate the well-known difficulties and obstacles involved in self-awareness and relating it integrally to one's intellectual inquiries, and the never-ending and decidedly imperfect character of the results. I can only attest here to the indispensability and the enrichment of making the attempt, and suggest some questions I believe everyone who participates in theological reflection should ask herself or himself. One set of questions is directed toward the content of one's theology: What are the main theological themes with which I have been preoccupied? What elements in my own life-history may have played a role in choosing to emphasize those themes and not others? Who are my theological "heroes"? What is it I admire about them--their themes, their methods, their style, their *persona*, their life-experience? Why do they strike responsive chords in myself? Who are my theological "villains," and why? Why do I simply tend to ignore some thinkers and movements that are obviously worthy of attention? What are the elements of rationalization in the reasons I give for my theological likes, dislikes, and indifferences?

Another set of questions might focus on my education as a theologian: Where did I do my graduate theological education (perhaps undergraduate work as well), and why did I choose to do it there? If I spent all or part of my graduate theological education in a denominational or a non-demoninational institution, what specific sorts of limiting and biasing influences might that have had? Which faculty members was I drawn to, which ones was I not, and why? What schools of thought were represented in my graduate institution, what stance did I take toward them (adherence, critical distance, aloofness, negative reaction), and why? What factors were involved in my having specialized in one area rather than another (the contingent elements in this sort of crucial career decision can be quite remarkable, as I know from my own students)? How might that focussing have cut me somewhat off from and reduced my sympathy with certain other areas or disciplines that I should on objective grounds acquire some basic knowledge of and take more seriously? What are my rationalizations for not doing so? In what ways generally has my experience of graduate education shaped the selectivities of my theological career?

Working progressively "inward" in my theological self-analysis I come to a third set of questions that ground all the rest. How would I describe myself characterologically in terms of various dipolar personality emphases: hard/soft, rigid/flexible, logical/intutitive, active/contemplative, cool/excitable, abstract/concrete, extravertive/intravertive, moralistic/ antinomian, open/guarded, compulsive/impulsive, aesthetic/prosaic, optimistic/pessimistic, social/individualistic, idealistic/ realistic? What are the themes of my night dreams and my daytime fantasies? What are the persons like with whom I have entered into the closest relationships? What are my most tenacious compulsions, my deepest secrets, my greatest anxieties? What relationships, events, and contexts in my earliest years and childhood seem to have been the most important in molding me into the sort of person I have become with the sorts of interests and concerns I have--parents, siblings, traumatic illnesses, family tragedies, socio-economic and cultural environment, schooling? What about the clearly enormous and very largely unconscious role that the constitutional givens and cultural definitions of racial and sexual identity play in my whole sense of the world and thereby in my theological reflection? What connections can I discern between all these personal characteristics and my theological preoccupations?

The questions above are intended as a stimulus to consideration of the importance of self-analysis in theological reflection and, I hope, to some self-analysis on the part of my readers. Clearly the sorts of self-examination suggested by my questions are an exhaustive and never-ending process of critical self-discovery. For most of us a really deep and thorough analysis would require the help of a skilled analyst or therapist. But I believe that many of us can on our own cultivate sufficient detachment, honesty, and perceptiveness about ourselves to gain both personally beneficial and theologically critical self-knowledge.

Among seekers after truth and within the academic community, theologians have a distinctive advantage and opportunity. Their advantage is the fact that the inescapably autobiographical elements in their presuppositions and pursuits are patently "upfront". These elements can be suppressed or ignored only by a form of what Sartre called "bad faith"--a resonantly apposite term in speaking of theologians. Cultivating a healthy self-awareness and self-criticism, their opportunity is thereby to play a therapeutically critical role with regard to what they see going on among colleagues in other disciplines. Theological candor may in a modest way take an active part in holding before all inquirers a mirror that reveals the human faces our knowledge wears.

Chapter 9

On Not Worrying About "Faith": Christian Identification as an Empirical Reality

The Christian tradition has been incessantly and obsessively preoccupied with defining, commending, and evaluating faith--as even a cursory look at the entries under that heading in a good theological library will illustrate. In this essay I want to suggest that the whole enterprise has always been an inherently problematic and misguided one, and never more so than in the post-Enlightenment period of Christian history. I want to propose as a more illuminating, fruitful, and "objective" focus the empirical reality of people's observable *participation in* and *identification with* Christian communities, which manifests itself in a truly bewildering variety of ways. I do not flatter myself that the approach I am commending is new. I simply think that the point needs making periodically, since theologians continue to talk about faith and occasionally to write systematic theologies, and clergy and lay people keep expending religious energy on the subject.

1.   The problems of definition, description, and dislocation

Of the making of many definitions of faith there has been no end in Christendom. The standard ones in Western theology and philosophy of religion, classical and contemporary, are familiar. Faith is:

--willing assent of the intellect to certain propositions set forth as true on divine authority (Aquinas, traditional Catholicism, some forms of fundamentalism);

--personal trust in the reality of the unseen personal God, whether as grace-filled response or as "leap" beyond reason (Luther, Kierkegaard, much modern Protestant thought);

--a life-wager on the greater likelihood of Christianity's (or theism's being true than atheism or skepticism (Pascal, James);

--the state of being grasped "at the center of one's being" by a concern which is not merely proximate but ultimate or unconditional (Tillich);

--openness to the future as freedom from bondage to the past through a new understanding of one's existence (Bultmann);

--a way of "seeing" or "picturing" the world and human experience which, like all such basic perspectives on things, is ultimately unrationalizable (Wittgenstein, Hick).

While there is certainly some overlapping here, there is also a range of different emphases that are difficult to reconcile one with another. The fact that historically there has developed such a variety of characterizations of faith, each with a certain claim to at least partial plausibility, suggests at the outset the possibility that the concept itself is either indeterminately elastic or inherently problematic. The difficulty is reinforced when we try to use the definitions to describe what actually goes on among those who have called themselves Christians, participating in the tradition quite diversely from out of differing historical-cultural contexts and personal histories.

The definitional and phenomenological problems in turn expose a theological irony which we might call "dislocation." The traditional theological preoccupation with developing a norm or standard of "faith" by which to evaluate human responses to God involves a fateful shift of focus which the Protestant Reformation brought decisively to light: Beginning with the affirmation of the sovereignty and priority of divine grace and the profound ambiguity of human motivation and action, Christian thought repeatedly falls into a fixation precisely on the nature and content of human appropriation of divine grace. Historically we can see these lapses in the slide from St. Paul to the Dutero-Pauline literature and from the early Luther to Lutheran confessionalism and scholasticism. In modern theology it was Karl Barth who, to his lasting credit, saw more clearly than anyone else what was really at stake, boldly reaffirmed the absolute priority of revelation and grace and thoroughly relativized (although he certainly did not stop talking about) faith. His correction of his mentor Kierkegaard and his debates with his existentially preoccupied contemporaries Bultmann and Tillich are instructive on this question.[1]

So it appears to me that from three directions--conceptual, phenomenological, and theological--there are questions that must be directed at the ways in which Christian thought has talked about faith. In the following two sections I want to elaborate further these questions by highlighting, first, the causal and contextual factors that render the traditional focus on faith misplaced; and second, the spectrum of contemporary forms of participation in the Christian community that suggests a more useful way to approach things.

2. Priorities and perplexities: the inherent pluralism of the Christian religious situation

There are two bases for an approach that bypasses the emphasis on faith and focusses instead on the rich plurality of ways in which human beings find themselves related to Christian tradition and community. The first consists of the *theological* priority of the divine activity in self-disclosure and human salvation; the *historical* priority of the foundations and many-faceted heritage of the biblical and Christian traditions; and, inseparably related, the *social* priority of the community of Christians across space and time. Grace, tradition, and community are, on Christian theological terms themselves, the large divine and human contexts within which individual human responses are played out. These prior contextual factors play a decisive role in shaping those responses in all their infinite nuance and variation, in combination with the vagaries of individual temperament and experience.

A second basis for taking a pluralistic and empirical approach is the perplexities or ambiguities in the Christian message itself. Modern historical-critical

---

[1]On the Barth-Bultmann debates see, e.g., Eberhard Busch, *Karl Barth: His Life from Letters and Autobiographical Texts*, translated by John Bowden (Philadelphia: Fortress Press, 1976); and James D. Smart, *The Divided Mind of Modern Theology: Karl Barth and Rudolf Bultmann, 1908-1933* (Philadelphia: The Westminster Press, 1967). An interesting presentation of the issues between Barth and Tillich is Alexander McKelway's *The Systematic Theology of Paul Tillich: A Review and Analysis* (Richmond: John Knox Press, 1964).

study of the biblical literature has abundantly demonstrated that both the Hebrew Bible and the New Testament present many diverse theological strands. Faith itself is characterized in a wide variety of ways. In Rudolf Bultmann's classic essay on *pistis* (faith) in the Kittel-Friedrich *Theological Dictionary of the New Testament*, he detailed the range of meanings of the term in the New Testament writings. Among the common uses in the early Christian communities, it meant believing God's words, obedience, trust, hope, faithfulness, acceptance of the *kerygma*, a personal relation to Christ, and the Christian message itself (*fides quae creditur*). To these Paul added such distinctive nuances as a new self-understanding, a radical decision of will, an eschatological attitude, and a surrender of self-assurance. He also emphasized that faith was capable of different grades and individual possibilities, as in "growth in faith," "weakness in faith," and "fullness of faith." The Johannine literature in turn added its own special meanings: faith is renunciation (in the sense of "desecularization") of the world, an abiding in God's Word, and reception of Jesus' love.[2] Even allowing for overlapping, there is a range of meanings here that is not easily reduced to "a" meaning. Furthermore, since the New Testament writings are addressed to Christians in community and their style is proclamatory and hortatory, we find no real indication of what the psychological and behavioral "cash value" of these senses of faith is in the case of specific individuals.

Our knowledge of the transcendent in the biblical literature is entirely through the medium of interpretative human witness, and we know full well that that witness is bewilderingly multiform. When we add to that the large hermeneutical diversity of interpretation of the biblical literature by succeeding generations of Christian theologians in response to changing cultural and historical circumstances, it further reinforces the suspicion that perhaps the efforts to discover "the" meaning of faith are the misguided pursuit of a will-o'-the-wisp. The biblical writings and their historical and contemporary interpretations reflect that same theological, social, and individual diversity that militates against the usual monochromatic emphasis on faith as the key to understanding Christian existence.

---

[2]Gerhard Friedrich, ed., *Theological Dictionary of the New Testament*, vol. VI, translated and edited by Geoffrey W. Bromiley (Grand Rapids: Wm. B. Eerdmans Publishing Company, 1971), 174-228.

3. The contemporary spectrum of Christian identification

As sociologists of religion such as Peter Berger have long pointed out, privatization and pluralism are hallmarks of religion in the modern secularized world.[3] The proliferation and civil toleration of all sorts of Christian as well as other religious groups in the Western world, together with the individualism of modern life, have dramatically reinforced and extended the diversity of ways in which people relate themselves to the Christian tradition. On doctrinal matters (often included under the rubric of faith) many Christian denominations have become so latitudinarian that "heresy" has become an obsolete term. In those for which "right doctrine" is still officially an important issue, as for example Roman Catholicism and certain Lutheran bodies, investigations of the orthodoxy of clergy and theologians and heresy trials are popularly viewed as anachronistic denials of personal liberty and integrity.[4] The range of opinion and practice within any denomination is greater than that between denominations. All this has taken place, furthermore, within the context of the dramatic developments in human knowledge that have marked modern Western history since the Scientific Revolution. Their equally dramatic effects on the Christian churches and their self-understanding have produced among reflective Christians generally a chastened recognition of the diversity and the finiteness of our grasp of what concerns us ultimately.

The result of all this is a mind-boggling range of attitudes and activities that identify themselves as "Christian" in the late twentieth century. The spectrum ranges from maximal to minimal intensity, from absolute certitude to radical doubt. At one end, for example, is the person who believes that she or he has direct personal experience of the presence of God in Christ. At the other end is the person who, amid serious intellectual doubts and vacillating uncertainty about the truth of Christianity and what he or she believes, continues to participate in the Christian community as both a heritage and a source of insight, renewal, and challenge. In

---

[3]See, e.g., Peter L. Berger, *The Sacred Canopy: Elements of a Sociological Theory of Religion* (Garden City: Doubleday & Company, Inc., 1969), especially chs. 5-7.

[4]In the Epilogue to his informative monograph *The Ethics of Belief: An Essay on the Victorian Religious Conscience* (Tallahassee: American Academy of Religion, 1974), James C. Livingston describes and laments the complete erosion of moral concern in the Church of England over the problem of theological integrity about which the Victorians were so earnestly exercised (57-60).

between is a range of types which involve greater and lesser degrees of assurance, feeling, and reason.

Especially striking in contemporary Christian life and thought are modes of participation that combine the most radical sorts of criticism of the tradition with active commitment to its continuing viability. While of course the heritage of prophetic criticism within the Jewish and Christian communities is as old as ancient Israel, in some of its modern forms it can espouse an intellectual skepticism and thoroughgoing "revisionism" that represent a much more foundational challenge. Two good examples from the past twenty-five years are the widely misunderstood and caricatured "death of God" theologies and the current feminist theologies. Attempting to describe the "faith" of, say, the feminist socialist Christian ethicist Beverly Wildung Harrison alongside the "faith" of Pope John Paul II dramatically points up the inadequacy of the standard theological preoccupation with defining faith and the need for a shift of focus.

As someone who has moved in liberal religious circles for some years, I am frequently struck by what I see at the "left" end of the Christian spectrum generally. Liberalism is of course typically tentative, open-ended, and dominated by modern knowledge in its theological formulations. But liberal forms of Christianity range over a spectrum of their own which at one end is a robust rational theism and at the other end shades off into sheer agnosticism.

Paul Tillich's well-known description of the situation of the modern theologian is apt as a description of many reflective Christians:

> . . . Being inside the circle, he must have made an existential decision; he must be in the situation of faith. But no one can say of himself that he is in the situation of faith. No one can call himself a theologian, even if he is called to be a teacher of theology. Every theologian is committed *and* alienated; he is always in faith *and* in doubt; he is inside *and* outside the theological circle. Sometimes the one side prevails, sometimes the other; and he is never certain which side really prevails. Therefore, one criterion alone can be applied: a person can be a theologian as long as he acknowledges the content of the theological circle as his ultimate concern. Whether this is true does not depend on his intellectual or moral or emotional state; it does not depend on the power of regeneration or the grade of sanctification. Rather it depends on his being ultimately concerned

with the Christian message even if he is sometimes inclined to attack
and to reject it.[5]

Interestingly, "ultimate concern" seems a more accurately descriptive term here than
"faith," despite the fact that Tillich himself equated the two. There are sensitive and
thoughtful persons formed by the Christian religious tradition who as mature adults
find themselves still wrestling with the issues and in the context of that tradition,
despite the most fundamental intellectual problems. They are "ultimately
concerned" with Christianity, but do they have "faith"? Perhaps even "ultimate
concern" is too strong a word for this phenomenon. It is a way of participating, a
means of identification, a mode of relating, a place to stand, an orientation, a
"style," even in a certain sense a "way of life"--but it is simply unnecessary and
confusing to insist on calling it "faith" or generalizing the meaning of "faith" so that
it applies to everything. We need a more neutral and empirical term to embrace a
Christian spectrum that includes a Jerry Falwell and a Thomas Altizer, a Mother
Teresa and a Rosemary Ruether.

4. A modest proposal

The term we want, as I have already suggested, is something like
participation in or *identification* with the Christian community and tradition. The
church, considered empirically, consists of those numerous, loosely connected,
motley groupings of people who in an enormous variety of ways participate in and
identify themselves with Christianity. I believe that the whole emphasis--both
theological and phenomenological--needs to be shifted away from the location and
definition of faith as certain sorts of individual, subjective orientation. In its place
we would do better to substitute an empirical focus simply on persons' participation
in the Christian tradition and community, which observably articulates itself in an
almost endless profusion of individual and communal, credulous and critical,
confident and skeptical forms.

Within this context of observable relationship, Christian groups and
theologians are certainly at liberty to say that some modes of participation are

---

[5]Paul Tillich, *Systematic Theology*, vol. I (Chicago: University of Chicago
Press, 1951), 10.

"better" and "worse," more and less "authentic"--always of course humbly and cautiously keeping in mind the sovereignty and priority of the One who alone knows the secrets of the human heart. But over against the historical plurality of expressions and definitions of faith, the model I propose has the advantage of being comprehensive rather than narrow, empirical rather than aprioristic, and contextual rather than individualist. It encourages a theological shift from the vagaries of individual belief and attitude to those aspects of the biblical literature and the Christian theological tradition which see in the *ecclesia*--the church or community of Christians--the primary reality in which people locate themselves in many different ways.

Bibliography of Works Cited

Arnold, Matthew. *God and the Bible: A Sequel to "Literature and Dogma."* Edited by R. H. Super. Vol. 7 of *The Complete Prose Works of Matthew Arnold*. Ann Arbor: University of Michigan Press, 1970.

_____. *Literature and Dogma: An Essay Towards a Better Apprehension of the Bible*. New York: AMS Press, 1970.

_____. "Literature and Science." In *Poetry and Criticism of Matthew Arnold*, edited with an introduction and notes by A. Dwight Culler, 381-396. Boston: Houghton Mifflin, 1961.

Axel, Larry. "Religious Possibilities Since 1945: An Empirical Approach." *Kairos: An Independent Quarterly of Liberal Religion* 29 (1983).

Barrett, William. *The Illusion of Technique*. Garden City, NY: Anchor Books, 1979.

Beckett, Samuel. *Waiting for Godot*. New York: Grove Press, 1954.

Berger, Peter. *The Sacred Canopy: Elements of a Sociological Theory of Religion*. Garden City, NY: Doubleday & Company, 1969.

_____ and Thomas Luckmann. *The Social Construction of Reality*. New York: Anchor Books, 1967.

Bernstein, Richard. *Beyond Objectivism and Relativism: Science, Hermeneutics, and Praxis*. Philadelphia: University of Pennsylvania Press, 1983.

Bonhoeffer, Dietrich. *Letters and Papers from Prison*. The Enlarged Edition. Edited by Eberhard Bethge, translated by Reginald Fuller, Frank Clarke and others, with additional material translated by John Bowden. New York: The Macmillan Company, 1972.

Borowitz, Eugene. *A New Jewish Theology in the Making.* Philadelphia: The Westminster Press, 1968.

Bultmann, Rudolf. *"Pistis."* In *Theological Dictionary of the New Testament,* edited by Gerhard Friedrich, vol. 6, 174-228. Translated and edited by Geoffrey W. Bromiley. Grand Rapids, MI: Wm. B. Eerdmans Publishing Company, 1971.

Busch, Eberhard. *Karl Barth: His Life from Letters and Autobiographical Texts.* Translated by John Bowden. Philadelphia: Fortress Press, 1976.

Camus, Albert. *Lyrical and Critical Essays.* Translated by Ellen Conroy Kennedy, edited and with notes by Philip Thody. New York: Alfred A. Knopf, 1968.

_____. *The Myth of Sisyphus and Other Essays.* Translated by Justin O'Brien. New York: Alfred A. Knopf, 1955.

_____. *The Plague.* Translated by Stuart Gilbert. New York: Modern Library, 1948.

_____. *The Rebel: An Essay on Man in Revolt.* Translated by Anthony Bower with a Foreword by Sir Herbert Read. New York: Random House, 1956.

Chesterton, G. K. *The Father Brown Omnibus.* New York: Dodd, 1983.

_____. *Orthodoxy.* London: The Bodley Head, 1908.

Condorcet, Jean Antoine de Caritat, Marquis de. *Sketch for a Historical Picture of the Progress of the Human Mind.* Translated by June Barraclough. New York: Noonday Press, 1955.

Cupitt, Don. *Only Human.* London: SCM Press, 1985.

_____. *Taking Leave of God.* London: SCM Press, 1980.

_____. *The World to Come.* London: SCM Press, 1982.

Daly, Mary. *Beyond God the Father: Toward a Philosophy of Women's Liberation.* Boston: Beacon Press, 1973.

Dewey, John. *A Common Faith.* New Haven: Yale University Press, 1934.

Driver, Tom. *Christ in a Changing World: Toward an Ethical Christology.* New York: Crossroad, 1981.

Eliot, George. *Scenes of Clerical Life.* New York: Oxford University Press, 1988.

Fiorenza, Elisabeth Schüssler. *Bread Not Stone: The Challenge of Feminist Biblical Interpretation.* Boston: Beacon Press, 1984.

Flew, Antony *et al.*, "Theology and Falsification." In *New Essays in Philosophical Theology*, edited by Antony Flew and Alasdair MacIntyre, 96-130. New York: The Macmillan Company, 1955.

Flint, Robert. *Agnosticism.* New York: Charles Scribner's Sons, 1903.

Frankenberry, Nancy. *Religion and Radical Empiricism.* Albany: SUNY Press, 1987.

Freud, Sigmund. *The Future of an Illusion.* Translated and edited by James Strachey. New York: W. W. Norton & Company, 1961.

Greene, Graham. *A Burnt-Out Case.* New York: Penguin Books, 1977.

_____. *The End of the Affair.* New York: Penguin Books, 1977.

_____. *The Power and the Glory.* New York: Penguin Books, 1977.

Harrington, Michael. *The Politics at God's Funeral: The Spiritual Crisis of Western Civilization.* New York: Penguin Books, 1983.

Hepburn, Ronald. *Christianity and Paradox.* London: Watts, 1958.

Herberg, Will. *Judaism and Modern Man.* New York: Harper & Row, 1951.

Hick, John. *Christianity at the Centre.* London: SCM Press Ltd., 1968.

_____. *Death and Eternal Life.* New York: Harper & Row, 1976.

_____. "Eschatological Verification Reconsidered." *Religious Studies* 13 (June 1977): 189-202.

_____. *Faith and Knowledge.* Ithaca, NY: Cornell University Press, 1957.

_____. *God Has Many Names.* Philadelphia: The Westminster Press, 1982.

Holyoake, George Jacob. *The Reasoner* 30 (January 1871), 1.

Huxley, Thomas Henry. *The Essence of T. H. Huxley.* Selections from his writings edited with several brief introductory essays by Cyril Bibby. New York: St. Martin's Press, 1967.

_____. *Selections from the Essays.* Edited by Alburey Castell. Arlington Heights, IL: AHM Publishing Corporation, 1948.

James, William. *Essays on Radical Empiricism.* New York: E. P. Dutton, 1971.

_____. *Pragmatism and Other Essays.* New York: Washington Square Press, 1963.

_____. *The Will to Believe and Other Essays in Popular Philosophy.* Cambridge, MA: Harvard University Press, 1979.

Kahn, Herman. *The Coming Boom: Economic, Political, Social.* New York: Simon & Schuster, 1983.

Kant, Immanuel. "Idea for a Universal History with a Cosmopolitan Intent." In *Perpetual Peace and Other Essays,* translated, with Introduction, by Ted Humphrey. Indianapolis: Hackett Publishing Company, 1983.

Kaufmann, Walter. *Critique of Religion and Philosophy.* Garden City, NY: Doubleday & Company, 1958.

_____. *Existentialism, Religion, and Death: Thirteen Essays.* New York: New American Library, 1976.

_____. *The Faith of a Heretic.* Garden City, NY: Doubleday & Company, 1961.

Kierkegaard, Sören. *Fear and Trembling.* Translated, with an introduction and notes, by Walter Lowrie. Princeton: Princeton University Press, 1974.

_____. *The Gospel of Suffering.* Translated by A. S. Aldworth and W. S. Ferrie. London: James Clarke & Co., Ltd., 1955.

_____. *The Last Years: Journals 1853-1855.* Edited and translated by Ronald Gregor Smith. London: Collins, 1965.

Kuhn, Thomas. *The Structure of Scientific Revolutions.* 2nd ed. Chicago: University of Chicago Press, 1970.

Lewis, C. S. *The Four Loves.* New York: Harcourt Brace Jovanovich, 1960.

_____. *Mere Christianity.* London: Collins, 1952.

_____. *The Chronicles of Narnia.* 7 vols. London: Collins.

Livingston, James C. *The Ethics of Belief: An Essay on the Victorian Religious Conscience.* Tallahassee, FL: American Academy of Religion, 1974.

_____. *Matthew Arnold and Christianity: His Religious Prose Writings.* Columbia: University of South Carolina Press, 1986.

Mansel, Henry. *The Limits of Religious Thought Examined.*

McCarthy, Gerald D., ed. *The Ethics of Belief.* Atlanta: Scholars Press, 1986.

McFague, Sallie. *Metaphorical Theology: Models of God in Religious Language.* Philadelphia: Fortress Press, 1982.

McKelway, Alexander. *The Systematic Theology of Paul Tillich: A Review and Analysis.* Richmond, VA: John Knox Press, 1964.

Mill, John Stuart. *The Subjection of Women.* London: D. Appleton, 1869.

_____. *Three Essays on Religion*. New York: Greenwood Press. Reprint of 1874 edition.

Muggeridge, Malcolm. *Jesus Rediscovered*. New York: Doubleday & Company, 1979.

Niebuhr, H. Richard. *The Meaning of Revelation*. New York: The Macmillan Company, 1941.

Nietzsche, Friedrich. *Twilight of the Idols*. Translated, with an Introduction and Commentary, by R. J. Hollingdale. Harmondsworth, England: Penguin Books Ltd., 1968.

Novak, Michael. *Belief and Unbelief*. New York: New American Library, 1965.

_____. *The Experience of Nothingness*. New York: Harper & Row, 1970.

Phillips, D. Z. *Faith and Philosophical Enquiry*. London: Routledge & Kegan Paul, 1979.

Plaskow, Judith. *Sex, Sin and Grace: Women's Experience and the Theologies of Reinhold Niebuhr and Paul Tillich*. Lanham, MD: University Press of America, 1980.

Polanyi, Michael. *Knowing and Being*. Edited by Marjorie Grene. Chicago: University of Chicago Press, 1969.

Rorty, Richard. *Philosophy and the Mirror of Nature*. Princeton: Princeton University Press, 1979.

Ruether, Rosemary Radford. *Disputed Questions: On Being a Christian*. Nashville: Abingdon Press, 1982.

_____. *Sexism and God-Talk: Toward a Feminist Theology*. Boston: Beacon Press, 1983.

Sakharov, Andrei. *Alarm and Hope*. New York: Random House, 1978.

Santayana, George. *Reason in Religion*. *Works*, vol. 4. New York: Charles Scribner's Sons, 1936.

Sartre, Jean-Paul. *Being and Nothingness: An Essay in Phenomenological Ontology*. Translated and with an introduction by Hazel E. Barnes. New York: Philosophical Library, 1956.

_____. "Existentialism is a Humanism." In *Existentialism from Dostoevsky to Sartre*, edited by Walter Kaufmann, 345-369. New York: New American Library, 1975.

122

Schweitzer, Albert. *Out of My Life and Thought*. Translated by C. T. Campion. New York: Henry Holt and Company, 1933.

Smart, James D. *The Divided Mind of Modern Theology: Karl Barth and Rudolf Bultmann, 1908-1933*. Philadelphia: The Westminster Press, 1967.

Smith, Stevie. "Some Impediments to Christian Commitment." In *Me Again: Uncollected Writings of Stevie Smith*. Edited by Jack Barbera and William McBrien with a Preface by James MacGibbon. London: Virago Press, 1982.

Smith, Wilfred Cantwell. *The Meaning and End of Religion*. New York: Harper & Row, 1978.

Temple, Frederick *et al*. *Essays and Reviews*. Reprint of 1860 edition. Brookfield, VT: Gregg International Publishers.

Tillich, Paul. *Systematic Theology*. Vol. 1. Chicago: University of Chicago Press, 1951.

Trulove, Sarah Chappell and James Woelfel. "The Feminist Re-formation of American Religious Thought." In *Religion and Philosophy in the United States of America*, edited by Peter Freese, vol. 2, 748-753. Essen: Verlag die blaue Eule, 1987.

Twain, Mark. *Letters from the Earth*. New York: Harper & Row, 1974.

_____. *The Mysterious Stranger and Other Stories*. New York: New American Library, 1962.

Tzara, Tristan. "Dadaism." In *The Modern Tradition: Backgrounds of Modern Literature*, edited by Richard Ellmann and Charles Feidelson, Jr., 595-601. New York: Oxford University Press, 1965.

Van Buren, Paul M. *Theological Explorations*. New York: The Macmillan Company, 1968.

Voltaire. *Candide*. Translated by Lowell Bair. New York: Bantam Books, 1981.

Weil, Simone. *Waiting for God*. Translated by Emma Craufurd, with an Introduction by Leslie Fiedler. New York: Harper & Row, 1973.

Wieman, Henry Nelson. "John Dewey's Common Faith." *The Christian Century* (November 14, 1934), 1450-1452.

_____, John Dewey, and E. E. Aubrey. "Is John Dewey a Theist?" *The Christian Century* (December 5, 1934), 1550-1553.

Williams, Harry. "Theology and Self-awareness." In *Soundings: Essays Concerning Christian Understanding*, edited by A. R. Vidler. Cambridge: Cambridge University Press, 1962.

_____. *True Christianity*. Springfield, IL: Templegate Publishers, 1975.

_____. *True Resurrection*. New York: Harper & Row, 1972.

Winch, Peter. *The Idea of a Social Science and Its Relation to Philosophy*. London: Routledge & Kegan Paul, 1958.

Wittgenstein, Ludwig. *Philosophical Investigations*. Translated by G. E. M. Anscombe. New York: The Macmillan Company, 1953.

Woelfel, James W. *Augustinian Humanism: Studies in Human Bondage and Earthly Grace*. Washington: University Press of America, 1979.

_____. "Between Faith and Skepticism: A Case Study." *American Journal of Theology and Philosophy* 1 (1980): 1-13.

_____. *Bonhoeffer's Theology: Classical and Revolutionary*. Nashville and New York: Abingdon Press, 1970.

_____. *Borderland Christianity: Critical Reason and the Christian Vision of Love*. Nashville and New York: Abingdon Press, 1973.

_____. *Camus: A Theological Perspective*. Nashville and New York: Abingdon Press, 1975. Reprinted, with a new Preface by Richard Fleming, as *Albert Camus on the Sacred and the Secular*. Lanham, MD: University Press of America, 1987.

_____. "William James on Victorian Agnosticism: A Strange Blindness." In *God, Values, and Empiricism: Issues in Philosophical Theology*, edited by Creighton Peden and Larry E. Axel, 239-248. Macon, GA: Mercer University Press, 1989.